306.87 CHR
The complete book of
aunts /
Christiansen, Rupert
815232

Re Jul 10
WK Jan 2011

D1053650

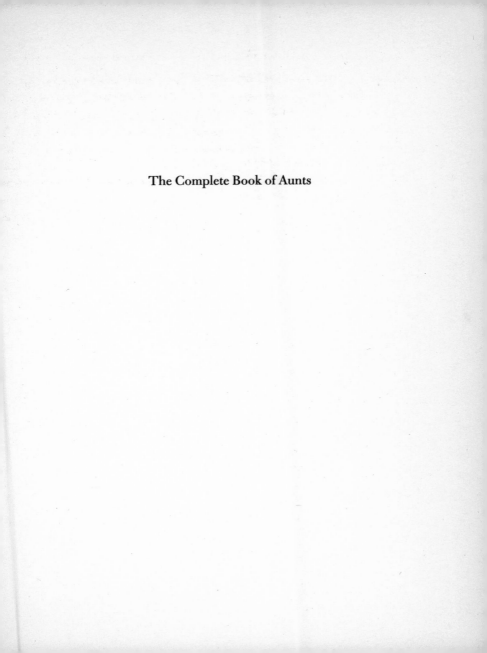

The Complete Book of Aunts

by the same author

THE FABER POCKET GUIDE TO OPERA
PRIMA DONNA
ROMANTIC AFFINITIES
PARIS BABYLON
THE VISITORS
ARTHUR HUGH CLOUGH

The Complete Book of Aunts

RUPERT CHRISTIANSEN

ILLUSTRATED BY STEPHANIE VON REISWITZ

faber and faber

For my sister Anna,
and in memory of J. M. M. and K. G. C.

First published in 2006
by Faber and Faber Limited
3 Queen Square London WC1N 3AU

Typeset by Faber and Faber Limited
Printed in England by Mackays of Chatham, plc

All rights reserved
© Rupert Christiansen, 2006

The right of Rupert Christiansen to be identified as author of this work
has been asserted in accordance with Section 77 of the Copyright,
Designs and Patents Act 1988

A CIP record for this book
is available from the British Library

ISBN 978–0–571–22655–9
ISBN 0–571–22655–8

4 6 8 10 9 7 5

Contents

Aunt Janet

At the committal service, the vicar gathered us round a raw square hole in the ground and asked if anyone wanted to place Janet's casket of ashes in the grave. I had loved my aunt deeply and I owed her much. Family seniority also required me to volunteer, but my nerves paralysed me and I stood rooted to the spot. My sister, braver and wiser than I am, stepped forward without any fuss and laid her to rest. I don't know how she managed: even in the crematorium I had come close to abject blubbing, squeezing my eyes shut when that dismally theatrical curtain was drawn across the plinth and the organ oozed out its pieties. Farewell, Godspeed, most auntly of aunts.

Hers was not a dramatic existence, nor her story a particularly complex one, but it resonates with something George Eliot writes in *Middlemarch*: 'If we had a keen vision and feeling of all ordinary human life, it would be like hearing the grass grow and the squirrel's heart beat, and we should die of that roar which lies on the other side of silence.'

Gentle, patient, tolerant, loyal, watchful over those she loved and in her latter years increasingly batty and infuriating, my Aunt Janet had died at the ripe old age of eighty-five, after an 'ordinary human life' which rounded off with four miserable months in hospitals and convalescent homes. Her terminal condition had been variously diagnosed – heart trouble, a stroke, slow-growing cancer – but my guess is that she simply faded away from the lack of any compelling reason to continue. She was never much of a fighter, always preferring life to blow her where it listeth, and on the last occasion my sister and I saw her, we realized that she was quite calmly dying – she said as much several times, without concern – accepting it as self-evident.

I like to think she felt complete. She had fallen into a coma almost immediately after she had rallied enough to be taken gingerly out of hospital for lunch. In a quiet country pub on a warm summer's afternoon, she sipped a glass of wine and swallowed a few mouthfuls of food, taking doddering pleasure in her surroundings and the company of her family.

A few days later, she went. Appropriately for someone so auntly, her deathbed was attended by her niece, my cousin, who reported that she rose up and smiled with something like joy before her head fell back on the pillow and she passed away – where to, I would like to know. My mother, her sister, to whom she was closely if imperfectly attuned, was later visited several times in the night by an inexplicable cool breeze which blew softly about her head and then evanesced. We know that this is Janet's spirit, drifting back in her unassertive way from the other side to let us know that she is at peace and that, as Julian of Norwich affirmed, all shall be well and all manner of thing shall be well. If this sounds maudlin, I don't care; it's what we felt.

After the casket had been buried, we straggled back to her modest cottage for a wake. Aunt Janet had many friends in the Suffolk village in which she had lived for thirty years, and the tone of the proceedings was warm yet unsentimental. Two stout elderly ladies flirted coyly with the vicar, who got squiffy, and a retired naval commander bored for England on the decline of our armed forces. Eventually, when the bottles were empty, the mourners departed, most of them taking a token keepsake with them. We cleared up, and sat numbly in the silence.

The next morning, my sister and I, her executors, opened the box containing her papers. A cursory rummage made it clear that despite the austerity of her outward circumstances, she had squirrelled away a considerable amount of money, the great bulk of it bequeathed to her nephews and nieces. I can honestly say that at that point I was much more thrilled about something else: in an envelope addressed to me, I found a lovingly preserved programme for the Aldeburgh Festival 1953, which she had visited. Music being my great passion, it was the most beautiful and auntly gift I could have imagined – a reminder of our bond, and the embodiment of many long conversations about Britten and E. M. Forster and string quartets and the theatre and what life had been like in those grim yet optimistic days of post-war reconstruction.

The next morning we locked up the cottage and left it without regret. It was a bleak little place, in the middle of a sprawling yet isolated village of no palpable charm. Aunt Janet was not puritanical, but she had no sensitivity to personal comforts or interest in material possessions. More out of force of habit than pleasure, she drank whisky and smoked steadily: perhaps these practices numbed her to the penitential nature of her surroundings. There were no radiators, and the storage heaters were so tepidly ineffectual you wondered why they bothered. Hot water came dribbling reluctantly out of an Ascot boiler above the sink. Apart from an Ercolesque suite, upholstered in dirty oatmeal and pockmarked with cigarette burns, the furniture was stolidly Victorian. Sideboards contained stacks of useless inherited cut glass, crockery and cutlery; shelves and mantelpieces were covered with knick-knacks which provided neither ornament nor function. Nicotine-tinged walls were hung with anodyne pastoral scenes and family photographs. The bathroom was freezing, a crossroads for draughts and not a place to linger in a state of undress. A Dyson vacuum cleaner, standing in the hallway as if not yet feeling quite at home, struck an almost shockingly modern note.

Her clothes – well, we took them all to the charity shop. Most poignantly, by her bed, on a white melamine chest of drawers, sat the lifelines: blister packs and bottles of pills, a telephone, a reading light, paper tissues and a Bible, with a bookmark in Ecclesiastes 7 – 'A good name is better than precious ointment.' In her later years, she had become a communicant member of the Church of England, but my guess is that she clung to Christianity by her fingernails. When I recommended her to read A. N. Wilson's fascinating biography of St Paul, she looked very alarmed. 'I don't want anything to shake my faith,' she muttered.

She had a good name, however, being truly moral in a strong and unhypocritical way. Quite simply, she lived by her values: those long-lost Anglican, English, Home Front, Home Service values relating to tactful honesty, mind-your-own-business neighbourliness, good humour, self-respect and emotional continence. She saw right and wrong clearly, balancing pity and sympathy with distaste and disgust. Her principles were firm without being rigid. 'I have no time for such nonsense' was one of her favourite phrases, applied with equal dismissiveness to the bleeding-heart sentimentality of Tony Blair and the Princess of Wales as to the hanging-and-flogging brigade.

Although I never heard her make overtly harsh judgements of individuals, her silences left one in no doubt as to what she thought. If something she deplored appeared on the television – *The Vicar of Dibley*, for example – a down-the-nose look of disdainful hauteur would set in, and very chilling it was too. Once I took her to the ballet at Covent Garden. I thought naively that she would love the spectacle and grandeur of it all, but it was soon evident that she was quite unimpressed. She was similarly indifferent to lunch at my club and the sight of a minor television celebrity showing off at the next table. I used to work for a glossy magazine and thought it great fun. Without her ever saying a word, I was made stingingly aware that she despised my involvement in such extravagant, snobbish frippery, regarding it as unworthy of her family's name, the honour of which she protected like a lion.

Books that I published were therefore greeted with more respect, as worthy contributions to the ancestral annals, but she was never gushing in her praise. I was only doing what I had a duty to do, given my privileged circumstances, and her letters in response to the autographed copies I always sent her, though warm and encouraging and invariably bearing evidence of close reading, were also faintly chastening: this is all very well, she implied, but you could still do better. What she enjoyed seizing on was some minor detail – mention of a name or place – that fitted the jigsaw of her own experience and memory. For example, 'On page 143, you mention the village of Mickleham Parva. This rang a bell. I remember your grandfather visiting this place sometime before the war, where an old school friend of his was the Baptist minister. I think his name was Ernest Corrie.'

Does all this make her sound humourless, solemn? Well, she wasn't, not in the least. She had a ready sense of the ridiculous, and her tendency to wittering chatter and rambling reminiscence infuriated her sister, my mother, an altogether more focused and motivated personality. One whisky over her daily double and she would deliquesce into cascades of giggling: she adored stories of gaffes and misunderstandings, minor contretemps and small discomfitures and embarrassments. So, solemn, no; serious, yes.

Outwardly, her life had not been eventful. Born into a solidly middle-class Oxfordshire environment in the early 1920s, she did well at school and just before the war went on to become – as she was always proud to inform you – the youngest ever secretary at the Ministry of Works. It was a job she kept until VE Day, when she joined a smart estate agent. Her aspirations were limited to earning a seemly 9 to 5 living. She expected nothing of her job and didn't seem to mind that it entirely failed to stretch her good mind: what she really wanted was a man, a husband, a nest of security. But social timidity was her enemy here: she was reluctant to take any sort of initiative, and spent most of her evenings in London trailing in the wake of her more dashingly attractive younger sister, my mother, with whom she shared a room in a hostel for young ladies in Paddington. Anyone my mother fended off was passed on to Janet, who sat there, like a dog at a dinner table, waiting for scraps.

In 1948, she married a surveyor, Clive Whittle – a friend of an ex-boyfriend of my mother's – and went to live in Wymondham in Norfolk. Her family was grim-faced about the match, aware that Janet didn't love the man. But she was without illusions: in those days a respectable middle-class girl needed a husband, and in the aftermath of war, they were not so easy to find. She would get on with him and make the most of it. To quote George Eliot again, this time from *Felix Holt*: 'A woman can hardly ever choose . . . she is dependent on what happens to her. She must take meaner things, because only meaner things are within her reach.' Janet was of the last generation to live under that dispensation; my mother, being five years younger, found pushing herself that much easier. But for Janet, reaching beyond the meaner things would have taken a measure of heroism which she lacked.

Wymondham did not provide an auspicious start to married life. Clive Whittle's home was the large and dank Victorian pile off the high street in which he'd been brought up. In an upstairs flat lived his mother, a rather sinister, twisted old besom who clung to her son with fervour and must have resented Janet's intrusion. Like figures in a Daphne du Maurier melodrama, the two women would pass each other in corridors without a glance, as if the other did not exist, and I can't recall them ever eating at the same table, even on feast days. I cannot imagine what the point of schism could have been – Mrs Whittle's eternally moulting and stinking tomcat? – but one felt that something had been said in a Homeric confrontation that could never be forgotten or forgiven.

Janet made some friends, however, and took to her wifely duties in the quiet country town. It could have been worse, one supposes. Any cruelty, any hatred was buried and silent. She was not a prisoner, there were diversions, and nearby Norwich with its antiquities and tea shops was pleasant. She sat on committees, prompted for the amateur dramatic society, and eventually became a JP. She also read voraciously but critically, and greatly encouraged me in my own nascent bookishness. It was she who introduced me to Robert Louis Stevenson, for instance – I can vividly remember her whetting my appetite for *Kidnapped*, where my alter ego David Balfour grappled with miserly Uncle Ebenezer before running off with that noblest of head boys Alan Breck. We liked a little Shakespeare too, reciting 'When shall we three meet again' in weird-sister voices on car journeys and holding impassioned teatime readings of the murder of Julius Caesar and the tragical mirth of Pyramus and Thisbe.

One year she gave me *Northanger Abbey* for Christmas. I still have the copy, Wm Collins and Sons the publishers, 7s. 6d. the price. An odd choice, you might think, but actually one which showed exquisite auntly acumen and launched me on a lifetime's admiration of the matchless artistry and nous of another excellent English aunt with no time for nonsense, Jane Austen.

We visited Aunt Janet for a few days every year. The house in Wymondham gave me the creeps, in a thrilling way. Its warren of sculleries, pantries, attics, box rooms and back staircases were all filled with the distinctive smell of old Mrs Whittle's tomcat (or maybe of old Mrs Whittle herself) and presented endless possibilities for hiding and seeking and fantasies of ghosts and treasures and secret passages.

Whenever we arrived, Aunt Janet presented us with a special Famous Five tea – cucumber sandwiches, cupcakes, chocolate fingers, a Victoria sponge and a jug of iced Day-Glo orange barley water – served at the dining-room table, which was covered with the best linen cloth. After this welcoming spread, which seemed to have been produced at enormous effort, the

refreshments became dismally spartan: there was a peculiarly depressing sort of anonymous meat fricassée (mutton?) in a thick white sauce that was her standby, a greasy fried breakfast, and a rancid bread-and-butter pudding the thought of which makes me retch even now. (Food she always regarded as a necessity, a box of Milk Tray being her only sensual indulgence.)

There would be jaunts in the car to beauty spots, beaches, caves and stately homes, but a lot of the time I simply sat opposite Aunt Janet in short grey trousers and told her everything I knew and everything that had happened to me since we had last met. God knows how she endured it, but she did, remembering the names of farcically fat boys in my class, the notable marks I had received in exams, the false teeth and gammy leg of war veteran Mr Mee (scripture), the unjust punishments meted out by cruel young Mr Tanner (history), the ludicrous lisp of Mrs Parrinder (French), favourite Beatles tracks, my feats of ingenuity in the assembly of Airfix kits and Meccano. She listened, as it were, to the whole story of me, registering the nuances and refraining from judgements. I think that the realization that someone outside my immediate family circle could see me so clearly and see me whole gave me a valuable emotional confidence and a first lesson in the pleasure of intimacy – an aunt gift.

Meanwhile, she was desperately unhappy with Clive Whittle, though at the time I had no particular sense of this and he always seemed nice enough – a plump, affable film buff, with an intriguingly large hairy mole on his neck. After seventeen years, their marriage was annulled on the grounds of non-consummation. I do not know the reasons for this, nor do I wish to speculate. It must have been torture for both of them, and whatever their different anguish, it should be interred with their bones.

But she had fallen in love – at what stage, I am again unaware – with another Clive, Clive Hewson. He was a headmaster, divorced with three adult children, and a prominent figure in Wymondham. I know now that it was a long time brewing. One day, she unexpectedly came to stay with us. I came home from school, and there she was, unanticipated, weeding furiously in our tangled garden (she was good with flowers). She seemed *distrait* and her hands shook – what can she have been like when we were not there to inhibit her?

There was so much I wanted to tell her – my victory in the backstroke against Yardley Court, a play about a shipwreck that I had written with Gough, the glory of the Beach Boys' surfing safari – but my mother implied that I should lay off. I was eleven, it was 1966 and there were things I did not understand. The facts were: she had left Clive Whittle and was going to live somewhere else with Clive Hewson. A large bunch of red roses appeared via Interflora. I saw the accompanying card, which read: 'To my beloved wife, please come home.' She did not do so. Given her essential passivity and four-square morality, the decision to wrench herself away from Clive Whittle must have cost her enormous spiritual and emotional effort.

She and Clive Hewson, universally known on account of his rotundity as Pots, moved to Clanbury in Suffolk. After the annulment came through, they were married. It was too late for children, but Pots had three of his own, and she made as good a stepmother as she did an aunt. Pots taught at a grammar school; she worked part-time in a solicitor's office. They travelled around Europe in a variety of stately but unreliable old cars, ran the film club, built a group of friends, tended a garden far prettier than their house and made a decent, modest, righteous new life for themselves.

My mother was painfully divorced and needed to work. Unlike Janet, she was ambitious, talented and sophisticated, and she found success in the then new and glamorous profession of public relations. Her jobs often required her to travel abroad, and when our au pairs could not be expected to cope with her more extended absences, Janet was called upon. She came reluctantly, I feel, being a creature who disliked disruption and responsibility.

I vividly remember her arriving at the station, walking down the platform in her one good Jaeger coat, carrying a Revelation suitcase. (Why Revelation, I thought, what was there to reveal? When she died nearly forty years later, I found it in a cupboard. Lined with mouldy pink satin and a vanity mirror, it evoked a Proustian rush of memories.) Liberty Hall ensued. Without experience of children of her own, Janet had absolutely no idea how to discipline us in a regular manner, and cast-iron rules about bedtime and television-watching crumbled into glorious anarchy. The food under this non-regime was awful though. She would select a tin from the larder, empty its contents into a pan and turn on the gas. After some perfunctory stirring, she would transfer a pile of warm mush on to a plate. For pudding, there was a pink thing called Instant Whip, deliciously concocted of flavourings and additives. I think my mother's kitchen made her nervous.

One of these visits became the source of some acrimony. The moment my mother returned from New York, Janet was packed and ready to go; they literally met in the front hall. We children were banished upstairs, and we heard a lot of shouting, then even more ominous silences followed by the slamming of the front door. 'She expected me to take her to the station,' I heard my mother spit to a friend on the telephone later. 'All she cared about was getting back in time for Pots's birthday. Bloody selfish, that's what she is.'

Perhaps she was a bit. And so was my mother, and so was I. Jealousy of Pots entered into it. Although he was truly the nicest and most reasonable of men – a loyal but undogmatic

Labour supporter of the old school, who had served in Malaya during the war – he alienated Aunt Janet from me. Or so it felt: I was no longer the number-one man in her life. Possibly my lapse into dopey long-haired mumbling teenagerhood didn't endear me to her either.

But she never missed a birthday (cheques, of a periodically ascending sum) or Christmas (usually something she had knitted), and she continued to chart each step of my wayward progress. We had our bond, our conversation, our jokes and stock of literary allusions, one of our favourites, employed as an expression of outrage, being Lady Catherine de Bourgh's 'Are the shades of Pemberley to be thus polluted?' in *Pride and Prejudice*. For some reason, I thought this uproariously amusing. The trouble was that I still wanted her to myself, but on my terms. After the Beach Boys had come noisier and darker enthusiasms into which she couldn't follow me. The eleven-year-old who had wanted to tell her everything became a sixteen-year-old who wanted his life kept secret.

She and Pots enjoyed fifteen years of as much happiness as one can expect on earth. Then Pots's heart weakened and he became querulous and feeble and mercifully died quietly. Janet was stoical in widowhood – grateful, I think, to have had what she had – but something inside her shut down and she was never quite the same person again. She took to the church via a route I couldn't fathom, and as she declined into old age, her horizons steadily narrowed. She had always been thin and stooping, but now rheumatoid arthritis knobbled her hands and made her face ache and she became tetchy. She didn't moan, and she hated to be a bother. Her defensiveness made it all worse – she craved help but was too proud to accept it with

good grace. Beneath it all was a core of adamantine stubborn-
ness, as displayed in her refusal to take a taxi if there was even
the remotest possibility of a bus – or a lift. I hate to think of all
the discomfort she suffered in order to leave her nieces and
nephews money they did not really want or need. A genera-
tional thing, my friends tell me.

The balance of our relationship altered. Although she was
pleased when I dropped my ridiculous fantasies of going on to
the stage and became a writer instead, there was nothing she
could do to influence me now, and it was left to me to take the
initiative. I wish achingly that I had seen more of her in these
last years, but the drive to Clanbury was a bugger and her cottage unutterably joyless, so we kept urging her to come up to
London and stay at my mother's sunny and cushioned flat in
Highgate. We felt guilty about this, but providing extended
hospitality agitated and taxed her. Should she turn the heating
up or down? If I liked Earl Grey tea, she could get some in, but
she made do with PG Tips. Did I like pasta (or 'parsta', as she
called it), something which only entered her culinary reper-
toire late in life? Was the bed comfortable? (It wasn't.) Was I
bored? Did I want to use the telephone or the washing
machine? Because if so, just go ahead and don't even ask. Did
I know how grateful she was that I was bothering with an
infirm old lady like her? That was the question which made it
all so much worse.

Everything she owned was wearing out alongside her own
decrepitude, hence my surprise when I discovered that radiant
Dyson vacuum cleaner. The Christmas before she died, we
struggled one last time to the theatre – Pinero's *The Magistrate*, not very good – and then I took her to a little Italian place

for some 'parsta'. It was a quietly affectionate evening, even though her grasp of detail was weakening, and I think that she would have secretly preferred to avoid the *Sturm und Drang* of an evening out in the West End, not least as we returned to St James's Square to find that my humble car had been vandalized. 'Why do they do it?' she asked more in sorrow than in anger. 'What pleasure can it give them?'

Two months later, she fell badly and was taken into hospital, suffering more from confusion than broken bones. Clearly there wasn't anything much that could be done, and all one could hope was that she was free of pain or distress. My mother telephoned her almost daily, but her response was always vague and non-committal. The doctors shrugged politely: this was a case of nature taking its course, they rightly implied, and I'm glad they didn't attempt any violent reversal of her condition.

But visiting her was an ordeal: I worried that she would be so far gone that she wouldn't recognize me, and that would have been hard to bear. When I went into the ward and saw her sitting in a chair beside the bed, her expression glazed and her wizened frame clad in a faded winceyette St Michael nightdress that she must have bought in 1965, I feared the worst. On a table sat a filthy little mess of lunch that she had barely touched. She clutched my wrist as I sat down.

'Aunt Janet,' I said, 'you really should try to eat something.'

'I can't, dear, it's not very nice.'

'But you must eat something.'

She looked like a starved bird that had lost its feathers. 'So, what's the news?' she asked with an attempt at interest and the vestige of her sweet smile.

'Oh, nothing much. I think Tony Blair is in a lot of trouble.'

'I haven't read a newspaper for months,' she replied faintly.

'I was going skiing next week, but I've got so much work on that I've had to cancel.'

She stared at me benignly, and the purple, papery, arthritic claw that was once her hand pressed my wrist sympathetically. 'Are the shades of Pemberley to be thus polluted?' she quavered, in a voice which attempted to suggest the pomposity of Lady Catherine de Bourgh. It was hardly a relevant response to my skiing plight, but it didn't matter. I knew what she meant, as she had always known what it was that I meant. A week later, she died.

1

A Short History of the Aunt

'Why are there aunts?' asked a baffled four-year-old boy as I sat in his parents' dining room talking about this book over lunch. It's a question I cannot answer. Aunts are not ordained by nature; they do not exist in the animal world. (Elephant herds are matriarchal, and when the males are out of the way, the females band together to look after each other and nurture the cubs, even to the point of adopting any orphans. But these ladies are not necessarily blood-related; they are simply public-spirited.)

Anthropologists studying kinship patterns have had little to say about aunts. Not all societies recognize them – or at least, not all languages have bothered to develop a single word to describe a mother's or father's sister. Romany has only *sachi calli*, 'female relation', while separate words for aunt are almost non-existent in sub-Saharan Africa. In the extinct tongues of Old High German and Anglo-Saxon, the words *nevo* and *nift*, from which our 'nephew' and 'niece' are derived, appear to have been used to describe uncle and aunt *and* grandson and grand-daughter as well. Other peoples make careful distinctions between maternal and paternal aunts, in the interests of keeping lines, laws and customs of inheritance clearly defined. In Hindustani, for example, a paternal aunt is *phu-phi* and a maternal aunt *kala*; Latin has *matertera* and *amita*; and Scandinavian languages double up *tante* or *tant* with *faster* and *moster*.

In *The Development of Family and Marriage in Europe*, Professor Jack Goody writes: 'A kinship terminology that grouped together the siblings of both parents, placing each in the same category of "uncle" and "aunt" (though the holders of these roles were not inter-changeable in all areas of activity) developed first in Vernacular Latin in the late Roman Empire, then spread though the Romance languages, reaching England with the Norman Conquest.' But in English 'aunt', like 'cousin', continues to have a more general application as well: an aunt is not just the sister of one of your parents but any older woman with whom you are on friendly terms – an 'auntie'. It is in this latter sense that the aunt makes one of her rare appearances in the writings of William Shakespeare, when Puck boasts about his antics:

> The wisest aunt, telling the saddest tale,
> Sometimes for three-foot stool mistaketh me:
> (*A Midsummer Night's Dream*, II.i)

Where to begin? The Bible is uninterested in aunts. Homer and the Greek tragedians pretty much ignore them. The first aunt of any historical significance appears in ancient Rome. When Nero was three, his father Domitius died. Much to the fury of his atrocious mother Agrippina, who was exiled in disgrace, the boy was sent to live with his father's aunt Domitia Lepida. Being far from respectable, she proved a thoroughly bad influence, 'choosing a dancer and a barber to be his tutors', according to Suetonius.

When Claudius became Emperor in CE 41, both Nero and Agrippina were brought back to court. Agrippina loathed

Domitia Lepida and instigated a campaign of vilification against her, charging her with witchcraft. 'In beauty, age and wealth,' wrote Tacitus,

> there was little between them. Moreover, both were immoral, disreputable and violent, so they were as keen rivals in vice as in the gifts of fortune. But their sharpest issue was whether aunt or mother should stand first with Nero. Lepida sought to seduce his youthful character by kind words and indulgence. Agrippina, on the other hand, employed severity and menaces – she could give her son the Empire, but not endure him as Emperor . . .

On his accession to the throne in CE 54, Nero murdered Agrippina (thwarted incestuous passion being one putative motive) and then set about getting rid of Domitia Lepida too, hoping to inherit her fortune since she was childless. 'He found her confined to bed with severe constipation,' Suetonius gossips.

> The old lady stroked his downy beard affectionately – he was already full-grown – murmuring: 'Whenever you cele-brate your coming-of-age and present me this, I shall die happy.' Nero turned to his courtiers and said laughingly, 'In that case, I must shave at once.' Then he ordered the doc-tors to give her a laxative of fatal strength, seized her prop-erty before she was quite dead, and tore up the will so that nothing should escape him.

After this unforgettable scene, the records go very quiet on the matter of aunts for seventeen hundred years. Whether nephews and nieces were genuinely indifferent to them we cannot know, but certainly there is little evidence of any intense emotional relationships. Uncles fare no better. For some reason, this seems to change in mid-eighteenth-century England, when aunts become the objects of affection and gratitude. We hear about Catherine Perkins, who helped her nephew William Hutton become a bookseller, and the historian Edward Gibbon's devotion to his Aunt Kitty (see p. 34–6), while novels by Samuel Richardson and Fanny Burney paint vivid pictures of their heroines' aunts, who play more than passing roles in the story. In her fascinating book *Novel Relations*, Ruth Perry attempts to relate the rise of the aunt to a deep social change which took families away from a consanguineal to a conjugal model, in which loyalty towards your parents and 'extended' family became less important than loyalty towards your spouse and children – a phenomenon underpinned by the drive towards capitalistic independence and small businesses, with more people marrying younger and reproducing sooner.

Why should this make aunts more important? Because, Perry suggests, they were implicated in the question, urgently asked by young women especially, of the extent to which parents should be obeyed in the quest for marriage and the search for other adult figures who might support rebellion. This is certainly an obsessive theme of novels of the period, which repeatedly explore the idea of a girl fighting to marry the man she loves against the will of her tyrannical or uncomprehending parents, an issue made more urgent by the Marriage Act of 1753, which made it illegal for anyone under twenty-one to marry without their parents' consent. Who could a girl turn to for sympathetic, disinterested adult advice? Not a similarly inexperienced girlfriend but a wise old aunt with no axe to grind. Elizabeth Bennet's reliance on her companionable Aunt Gardiner in Jane Austen's *Pride and Prejudice* is only one example.

But this is only a theory, and a rather porous, tendentious one at that. Maybe it's better just to accept that suddenly it was time for aunthood to get its due. In the course of the next century or so, the familiar stereotypes emerge. The poet William Wordsworth's sister Dorothy is an early instance of the childless spinster aunt who grows up devoted to her big brother and then duplicates that love towards his offspring, in whose nurturing she plays a crucial role. Dorothy's particular care was the firstborn John, born with a 'noble forehead' that gave promise of a fine intellect. Alas, as Dorothy was forced to admit after attempting to home-school him, he turned out dim and obtuse. This made no difference to her love for him: she sewed him new suits and shirts when he went off to boarding school and prayed that 'God grant he may preserve his ingenuous dispositions.' Finally, he got into Cambridge, where he struggled to keep up. Appointed to a curacy in the wilds of Leicestershire, he begged his aunt to come and help him settle in. So she set off, cancelling an exciting holiday in Rome without a murmur of complaint.

'Nephews and nieces, whilst young and innocent, are as good almost as sons and daughters to a fervid and loving heart that has carried them in her arms from the hour they were born,' wrote Thomas de Quincey in his memoirs, presumably thinking of his friend Dorothy's poignant devotion to the hopeless John. 'But after a nephew has grown into a huge bulk of a man, six foot high, and as stout as a bullock . . . there is nothing in such a subject to rouse the flagging pulses of the heart and to sustain a fervid spirit.' Yet Dorothy was a loyal soul, and aunts can sustain their love on very little return: to be needed was sufficient joy.

The Victorian era was the aunt's finest hour, and the chapters which follow will detail several of their triumphs. Aunts (and this includes great-aunts) in the nineteenth century could be heroic figures, women who had avoided the surrender of marriage and sought spheres of activity beyond the roles of wife and mother. But chiefly they were objects of indulgent affection in a culture that sentimentalized the relics and recollections of childhood. E. M. Forster, for instance, wrote *Marianne Thornton*, a touching memoir in tribute to his great-aunt, a woman selflessly devoted to the cause of education who had died when he was barely seven. She had pampered and adored her little nephew, who at the time found her billing and cooing cloying and irritating. 'I was in the power of a failing old woman, who wanted to be kind but she was old and each visit she was older. How old was she? "Born in the reign of George the Fourth" my mother thought. "More likely Edward the Fourth" cried I.' When she died she left Forster £8,000, a sum which he described as 'the financial salvation of my life . . . she and no one else made my career as a writer possible'. The biography, his final book, was a pious attempt to repay a debt of love across the grave.

Aunts also become ripe for some good-natured ribbing. Such innocent expletives as 'My aunt!' or 'My sainted aunt!' date from the mid-nineteenth century (the expression of incredulity, 'My Aunt Fanny!' comes much later, according to

the *Oxford English Dictionary*). Aunt Sally was a fairground game, still popular in Oxfordshire pub gardens today, in which contestants aim eighteen-inch sticks at a six-inch dummy from a distance of ten yards – from which presumably springs the figurative use of Aunt Sally to describe a person or phenomenon that is a sitting duck for criticism or mockery. An Aunt Emma, in the quintessential Victorian recreation of croquet, is a player who obstreperously avoids risks and aims solely to impede the progress of others.

Late in the nineteenth century and into the early twentieth, aunts seem to have become even more emphatically comic figures, some of them merely amiably dotty, such as Aunt Etty in Gwen Raverat's *Period Piece* (see p. 131–3), and some of them figures of ludicrous self-importance and rigid propriety, such as Oscar Wilde's Lady Bracknell or P. G. Wodehouse's Aunt Agatha. The prim maiden aunt and the stingy old aunt became staple figures of theatrical farce and children's books, where they regularly make unseasonable appearances and unreasonable demands and usually soften up in the end. Uncles, it should be noted, have much less force, as either figures of authority or the butts of satire. In fact, uncles won't come into this book much at all, partly because so many notable aunts were unmarried.

After the Second World War, people began to tire of their aunts, identifying them with a discredited order of moral values and ramrod behaviour, a force for conservatism in an age desperate to break free of the catastrophic recent past. The BBC was sneerily nicknamed Auntie, in reference to its role as guardian of public decency, while in 1953, an essay by the playwright Terence Rattigan conjured up the figure of Aunt Edna as the embodiment of a certain sort of theatergoer who enjoyed a Shaftesbury Avenue matinee: 'a nice, respectable, middle-class middle-aged maiden lady with time on her hands' who 'does not appreciate Kafka' and is 'in short, a hopeless lowbrow'. Over the next decade, as Jimmy Porter ranted at the Royal Court and kitchen-sink drama took over from French-windows fluff, one could say that Aunt Edna became an Aunt Sally, enlisted by both radicals and conservatives.

Now, at the beginning of a new millennium, the great age of the aunt is over, at least in the western world. It lasted for about two hundred years, between the mid-eighteenth century and the mid-twentieth, greatly enriching our sense of family. Aunts continue to exist biologically, of course, but they have less potency in today's society. Younger women no longer want to be called aunt, with its stigma of prim middle age – which is just as well, since today's children are even more distinctly disinclined to use such an uncool word. For their part, children look to idiotic celebrities rather than their elder relations for their role models. The freedoms they have and their increased access to a wide range of experiences via the media mean that aunts can offer them less in the way of novelty and adventure.

In China, a nation whose citizens are encouraged to have no more than one baby and where male children are almost superstitiously favoured over females, the aunt must be classified as an endangered species. In Muslim and Hindu societies, where women have more definitely circumscribed territory and where the family remains a more cohesive institution and a more active moulder of lives than it does in Christian societies, she has a better chance of flourishing in her traditional role and identity. Quite what aunthood can mean in certain parts of west Africa, one cannot imagine: recent cases of horrific child abuse reported in London saw aunts from this background involved in the unspeakably vile torturing and eventual murder of nieces they deemed to be possessed of devils in need of exorcism.

A more edifying development in aunthood comes from the further reaches of medical technology, where it is now possible, thanks to egg donation, for a child's biological aunt to be his biological mother too (see p. 249–55 for Emma Davies's moving account of being the aunt to her son). Another remarkable case of this scientific legerdemain was reported in the British press in November 2005, when thirty-two-year-old Alex Patrick, left infertile as a result of cervical cancer, won the legal right to be recognized as the mother of a baby son who was the product of her husband's sperm fertilizing her twin sister's ovum, which was then carried through pregnancy by her elder sister. It was impossible not to be moved by this remarkable instance of unselfish sisterly solidarity, itself a bedrock of aunthood and the familial affections which fill this book.

Etymological Aunts

Most European languages use a one- or two-syllable word which appears to have derived from the Ancient Greek tethis *or the Latin* amita *and* tata, *a word meaning 'rearer' that could be assigned to a father (daddy?) or a wet nurse, as well as an aunt:*

Czech, Croatian: Teta
French, Dutch, German: Tante
Finnish: Tati
Italian: Zia
Russian: Tetya
Spanish/Portuguese: Tía
Turkish: Teyze

Further afield, 'aunt' is rendered:
Basque: Izeba
Guarani: Sy'y
Hungarian: Nagyneni
Kikuyu: Taata
Sanskrit: Nanandaa
Swahili: Shagazi
Welsh: Modryb
Japanese: Amitam *(rather alarmingly, the word for 'mother's sister' is the same as that for 'father's concubine')*

According to the Oxford English Dictionary, *aunt first appears in written English in around 1300, derived from the Old French* aunte *or* ante. *This usage survives today in the way that children are enjoined to call close but unrelated female family friends 'aunt' or 'auntie'. In the more louche periods of the seventeenth century, the word briefly entered smart urban slang as a term for prostitute, procuress or brothel-keeper.*

In sign language, 'aunt' is indicated by clenching the right hand and leaving the thumb facing upwards to form the letter A, then holding the hand close to your right cheek and shaking it slightly back and forth.

Oddities of French: 'tante' *is also a popular term of abuse for a homosexual, the equivalent of nancy-boy or pansy. 'Tatie' means 'most favourite aunt'; 'tatan' auntie.*

Oddities of English: although 'uncle' has been comfortably related to 'avuncular' since the 1830s, no equivalent adjective has ever evolved from 'aunt'. In this book, I am resorting to 'auntly', a word which, according to the OED, had only a brief and feeble currency: in 1844, Lady Lyttleton's letters send 'my best regards and Auntly bless-ings to my nephew', and two years later, Sara Coleridge's memoirs record 'a very motherly and auntly tale'. But it never caught on – why?

'Aunts'
by *Virginia Graham*

Children, when you have gone your several ways,
And have sought the long day's
Happiness, and the night's elusive dream,
Incredible as it may seem
You will turn, at some moment, like thirsting plants
To your aunts.
Now, aunts are not glamorous creatures,
As very often their features
Tend to be elderly caricatures of your own.
Aunts use eau-de-cologne
And live in rather out-of-the-way places,
And wear pointed white shoes with laces
Tied in a neat bow.
Ooh I know, I know!
Nevertheless I maintain that when you are old enough to
    learn pain,
are acquainted with sorrow, and know what fear is,
your aunts will not seem nearly such drearies,
you'll see,
believe me!
When you've broken off your engagement and want to
    hide,
you will go to Aunt Beatrice at Ambleside.
When the charwoman falls down dead,
Aunt Edith will give you a bed.
When your heart breaks, as hearts sometimes do,

Aunt Constance at Looe
will feed it on Cornish cream and philosophy,
soothe it with strawberries for tea;
and when, with the dew still behind your ears
you set forth to conquer wider spheres,
I do not think you will get much further the first night
than Aunt Maud in Shanklin, Isle of Wight.
Oh, yes, children, aunts are kind
and quite resigned
to the fact that you will not go near them for years,
and then bring them your tears.
Although at your tender age you resent their neglect of the
    Stage,
their inability to differentiate between jazz and swing,
and their poor reactions to Bing,
the day will dawn when they will rise up like rocks,
sheltering you with their long imprimé frocks
and cornflowered hats worn at such hopeless slants –
your nigh-forgotten, soon-remembered aunts.

   from *Consider the Years*

2

Mothering Aunts

When the meek and gentle Maria Brontë died in 1821, her last words were: 'Oh God my poor children oh God my poor children.' Six of them stood in a bleak, cold parsonage in the stony grey village of Haworth, on the moors of Yorkshire, with their stubborn, self-centred and emotionally troubled father. Maria, seven; Elizabeth, six; Charlotte, five; Branwell, four; Emily, three; Anne, one: over seven months, they had watched and heard their mother perish, in ever more excruciating pain. She might well feel anguish for their future.

To be left motherless is a universal human tragedy, one that draws the aunt out of the shadows to take centre stage in a bereaved family not quite her own. The role she must dutifully play is not always gratifying. She may be considered an intruder or branded second best. She may be required to sacrifice elements of her own life, nurturing nieces and nephews without access to the biological taproot of parenthood. To those who have known the intimate romantic sweetness of maternal love, she can assuage but never altogether compensate.

The Reverend Patrick Brontë suffered from his demons and did not warm easily to his offspring. He needed another wife but could not find one: three women he approached smartly rejected his unappealing offer. The alternative was his wife's sister, Elizabeth, who had nursed Maria in her dying days. She was over forty and had a home she liked in Cornwall, but her

Methodist piety meant that she could not find a way to refuse. So Aunt Branwell – the children always called her by her surname, a customary practice until the later nineteenth century – became the substitute, contributing her inherited annual income of £50 to the household and occupying a small bedroom which at first she shared with baby Anne.

She lacked charm and warmth, and never adjusted to Yorkshire ways. The servants found her 'a bit of a tyke . . . so crosslike an' fault finding, and so close'. Charlotte's lifelong friend Ellen Nussey remembered her more appealingly as 'a very small, antiquated little lady. She wore caps large enough for half a dozen of the present fashion, and a front of light auburn curls over her forehead. She always dressed in silk. She had a horror of the climate so far north, and of the stone floors in the parsonage . . . the social life of her younger days she used to recall with regret; she gave one the idea that she had been a belle among her own home acquaintances. She took snuff out of a very pretty gold snuff box, which she sometimes presented to you with a little laugh, as if she enjoyed the slight shock and astonishment visible in your countenance.'

As she grew older, the biting Yorkshire climate seems to have worn her down. She became increasingly strait-laced and reluctant to leave her bedroom, emerging only for a Sunday excursion to church, where her brother-in-law made a stern, unconsoling preacher. She kept her window bolted and the fire banked up to ward off the wind and the damp. Meals would be taken to her on a tray, and after mornings being schooled by their father, the children would be sent up to her every afternoon to sit still and do their duty.

Yet it was the cantankerous Branwell who appears to have been her favourite. He was certainly the one who grieved most when she died, recalling her as 'the guide and director of all the happy days connected with my childhood'. The three girls (Elizabeth and Maria both died as a result of the appalling rigours of a local boarding school) merely bowed to her yoke. Needle and thread were the fundamental elements of her daily regime, wielded, wrote another of Charlotte's friends Mary Taylor, 'with purpose or without . . . She used to keep the girls sewing charity clothing and maintained to me that it was not for the good of the recipients but of the servers. "It was proper for them to do it," she said.'

Aunt Branwell remained unaware of what went on when the children were alone downstairs: a secret ferment of imaginative life and the creation of the fantasy world of Gondal which later led Charlotte and Emily to produce three of the most powerful and original novels of the century. 'She was not her nieces' confidante,' Patrick Brontë admitted to Charlotte's biographer Mrs Gaskell when they discussed Aunt Branwell. But although her culture and her values were narrow, she had no instinct to interfere; as long as her rules and her routines were observed, she was not ambitious for power over her charges.

'She and her nieces went on smoothly enough,' wrote Mrs Gaskell, 'and though they might now and then be annoyed by petty tyranny, she still inspired them with sincere respect, and not a little affection. They were, moreover, grateful to her for many habits she had enforced upon them, and which in time had become second nature: order, method, neatness in everything; a perfect knowledge of all kinds of household work; an exact punctuality, and obedience to the laws of time and place

. . . with their impulsive natures it was positive repose to have learnt obedience to external laws.'

Nor was Aunt Branwell mercenary. In 1841, when Charlotte and Emily hatched a plan to train as teachers in Belgium and then return to take over Miss Wooler's school on Dewsbury Moor, Charlotte wrote to ask her for a loan. The letter certainly shows no whiff of intimidation. Indeed, given the limitation of her aunt's resources, Charlotte could be accused of a boldness bordering on arm-twisting. 'You always like to use your money to the best advantage. You are not fond of making shabby purchases; when you do confer a favour, it is often done in style; and, depend upon it, £50, or £100, thus laid out, would be well employed. Of course, I know no other friend in the world to whom I could apply on this subject, except yourself. I feel an absolute conviction that, if this advantage were allowed us, it would be the making of us for life. . . . I want us *all* to get on. I know we have talents, and I want them to be turned to account. I look to you, aunt, to help us. I think you will not refuse.' She did not, and Charlotte and Emily went to Belgium. Within months, however, Aunt Branwell had died from cancer, unrewarded and maybe unthanked for her steady, unspontaneous devotion.

She was given no way in: from the moment she arrived at Haworth, Aunt Branwell would have confronted a hexagonal web of delicate relationships and loyalties, consolidated over a deathbed. It was easier for Catherine Porten. When she inherited Edward Gibbon in 1747, his six siblings had all died, and only this one frail ten-year-old, with an outsize head and spindly frame, survived. He had not been close to his mother, and following her demise, he was delighted when his lugubrious and uncommunicative father sent him to live with her father and unmarried sister in a house near Putney Bridge. Recalling Aunt Kitty in his autobiography, he felt 'a tear of gratitude' trickling down his cheek. 'If there are any who rejoice that I live,' the historian of *The Decline and Fall of the Roman Empire* continued, 'to that dear and excellent woman they must hold themselves indebted.'

Unlike Aunt Branwell, Kitty was great fun, and she and the orphaned Edward shared tastes and interests. 'Her indulgent tenderness, the frankness of her temper, and my innate rising curiosity soon removed all distance between us.' Sceptical of ardent religion, she and the boy would engage in free moral discussion, and she introduced him to Pope's translations of Homer and the enthralling *Arabian Nights*. 'To my aunt's kind lessons, I ascribe my early and invincible love of reading, which I would not exchange for the treasures of India.' Under such tutelage, his health improved and his deformities faded. The roles of aunt and nephew dissolved: 'she was truly my mother, she became my friend'.

When at eighteen he got into some trouble over gambling debts, it was to her generosity that he applied for a bail-out: 'I know you have thoughts of doing something for me by your will, I beg you only to anticipate it . . . I tremble for your answer but beg it may be speedy.' It is a testament to the strength of their relationship that Kitty refused the plea, and Gibbon never resented her firmness. Throughout his life, she continued to be his 'dear Kitty', and he wrote to her with unfailing affection and candour. For her part, she took enormous pride in his literary achievements and lived on resiliently into her seventies, 'a giddy girl . . . never out of order above four and twenty hours at

a time . . . one of the youngest women I know about town.'
Sadly, she died in 1786, two years before the completion of
Decline and Fall. 'A good understanding, and an excellent
heart, with health, spirits and a competency; to live in the midst
of her friends till the age of fourscore and then to shut her eyes
without pain or remorse. Death can only have deprived her of
some years of weakness, perhaps of misery,' he reflected. 'All
this is perfectly true, but all these reflections will not dispel a
thousand sad and tender remembrances.'

This is the simplest case – a meeting of like minds uncom-
plicated by any severe test of loyalties, as neither party ever
married or was otherwise encumbered. For Mimi Stanley two
centuries later, it was more complicated. Her younger sister
Julia had married the feckless Alf Lennon, much to the dismay
of their respectable middle-class family. When Julia produced
a baby boy in 1940, Mimi went to see the child in hospital and
felt immediately that she was destined 'to be his mother'. She
chose the name John for him, with Julia patriotically adding
Winston to the certificate.

Five years later, when Alf had drifted off and Julia had taken
up with another man, Mimi insisted that she should take control of John and give him the proper stable family upbringing
that Julia was unable to provide. Julia meekly accepted, and
John moved to Mendips, a semi-detached house in Menlove
Avenue, Woolton, a pleasant Protestant suburb of Liverpool.
The mayor lived next door.

Mimi had trained as a nurse and then become a secretary. In
1939, she had married George Smith, a quiet, amiable dairy
farmer. They were very happy together, as far as anyone knows,
but because she had spent so much of her childhood looking

after her three younger sisters, Mimi let it be known that she did not want children of her own. Psychologists may see the appropriation of her sister's son in terms of displacement and surrogacy, but the simple fact is that Mimi loved John with a true enduring love that never faltered or softened. 'I would sometimes rant and rave at him, but deep down he knew I loved him and that he loved me,' she said. 'We were very close.' Love, love, love, all you need is love – and John Lennon was given plenty of it.

But it must have been muddling for the boy, being pulled in so many emotional directions. If strangers in the street took him for Mimi's son, she would not contradict them, yet he would also privately ask her: 'Why can't I call you Mummy?' He adored his Uncle George, but his biological father had effectively vanished. Meanwhile, in a strange inversion of nature, Julia became in effect his aunt, visiting regularly, sometimes daily, and lavishing him with indulgent affection and treats. Her second relationship produced two girls, John's half-sisters. None of this was clearly discussed or explained, and however anchored he was to his Mimi mummy (the assonance itself causing a further puzzle), John was consequently prey to a jumble of conflicting relationships and confusing presences and absences. The result was an anxious, anarchic, aggressive, ambitious, selfish, soft-hearted, crazy, mixed-up kid who led the local posse and fought and stole and swore and rode the bumpers of the tramcars when Mimi wasn't looking. He could well have turned delinquent, and jolly nearly did.

Within the walls of Mendips, however, things moved serenely and he was happy. Mimi was a conventional disciplinarian, emphasizing the value of domestic routine, cleanliness and good manners. She gave up work to rear John and proudly claimed that 'he never came back to an empty house'. He was required to mow the lawn, tidy his room and go to church on Sundays. His pocket money was five bob, and potted entertainment was limited to a trip to the pantomime at Christmas and the latest Walt Disney movie in the summer. Most significantly, it was a house with plenty of good books: John was consumed by *Just William*, *The Wind in the Willows* and *Alice in Wonderland*, and from the age of seven he began producing his own volumes of skits, cartoons and stories.

'My husband and I gave him a wonderful home,' Mimi claimed later, with justification. 'I never forgave my auntie for not treating me like a genius,' John later complained, only half-joking. But she always knew that he would 'amount to something', and he should have given her credit for providing the secure and comfortable environment from which he could mount a creative rebellion that would make him, fifteen years later, as famous as anyone on the planet.

Clearly a bright boy, he earned his 11-plus place at one of the best local grammar schools, Quarry Bank, a sensible, conservative institution which might have turned him into a doctor or a lawyer. Instead it unwittingly bred a nasty little so-and-so, the class comedian, lying and swearing and skiving off and cheeking the masters. 'I was aggressive because I wanted to be popular,' he told the Beatles' biographer Hunter Davies later. 'I wanted everybody to do what I told them to do, to laugh at my jokes and let me be the boss . . . It was all imagining I was Just William really.' Liberal application of the cane proved no deterrent, and Mimi came to dread the telephone ringing at home during the day, as the caller was usually the headmaster, complaining about the boy's latest misdemeanour. Having been ranked at the top of the first form, he ended up failing all his O-levels.

It was at Quarry Bank that music began to dominate John's imagination. Mimi had delighted in his wild drawings and verbal inventiveness, and it was this creative streak that she attempted to encourage. But Uncle George had started something when he slipped the boy his first musical instrument, an old mouth organ which he played incessantly. Mimi did not much like music and deplored what she considered a rubbishy noise, but his mother played the banjo and bought him a cheap £10 guitar and taught him some basic chords.

Mimi made him practise them out on the front porch. Later, she relented to the extent of buying him a superior £14 guitar, but she remained sceptical about his talent. 'Stick to art,' she told him, in what would become one of the most celebrated remarks in the Beatles mythology. 'The guitar's all right as a hobby, John, but you'll never make a living with it.'

It was the mid-1950s, an era in which the teenager, wriggling free of post-war privation and Puritanism, became the new social force, disruptive and disloyal. It was the era of rock 'n' roll, when popular music became pop and dance floors turned Dionysiac to the tune of Bill Haley and the Comets, Buddy Holly and the Crickets, and the sensual power of Elvis Presley. Infatuated with their vitality, John and some of his schoolfriends set up a crude skiffle band called the Quarrymen. One Saturday afternoon in 1956, they were playing at a church fête. Someone brought along a boy from the other side of the tracks – a Catholic council estate, to be precise – of whom Mimi, with her innocently snobbish insistence on respectability and the proprieties of caste, could never quite approve. His name was Paul McCartney.

Throughout the years of John's Teddy Boy delinquency, Mimi staunchly held the fort at Mendips. There were tragedies which the boy in his self-centred adolescent innocence never fully confronted – Uncle George dying suddenly, his mother being killed in a car accident – but Mimi's values remained immovable. She refused to countenance music as his destiny, made the plebeian Paul and George Harrison unwelcome in the house and pushed John into art college. He did no work at all there, as Mimi eventually intuited. One day she tracked him down to a dirty Liverpool dive known as the Cavern Club, where the band now calling itself the Beatles was playing in the lunch hour. She was appalled. 'Try as I might, I just couldn't get near the stage,' she recalled. 'If I could, I would have pulled him off it.' So she fought her way into his dressing room. 'Very nice, John,' she said, with grim sarcasm. 'This is very nice.'

In desperation, she signed him up to be a bus conductor, but he was nearly twenty and ready to take the first avenue of escape: the wild port of Hamburg, where the Beatles had been offered work in a club. For the time being, she had lost the battle. But when their first Hamburg gig came to an end, John went straight back to Mendips, throwing stones against Mimi's bedroom window in the middle of the night and shouting at her to let him in. He stormed upstairs, ignoring her lecture, and lay in his bedroom for a week.

For the next two years, until the advent of Brian Epstein and the big time, Mimi continued to exert what influence she could over her errant nephew, and at some level, her opinion, or at least her presence, continued to matter to him. He moved out, but the night before his shotgun wedding to Cynthia Powell, he came back to her and broke down in tears. Cynthia was a nice middle-class Protestant girl he had known since his art-college days, but Mimi realized that she was not his intellectual match and refused to attend the registry-office ceremony. (Later, the two women became close, staying together while the Beatles were touring.) John succeeded in persuading his aunt to listen to the band's first recorded single, 'Love Me Do', to which her response was a characteristic harrumph. 'If you think you're going to make your fortune with that, you've got another think coming.' 'Remember I said I'd be famous,' he retorted. 'What always worried me, John, was that you wouldn't be so much famous as notorious.' They were both right.

But once he had left home for good and the world was at his feet, singing his songs and laughing at his jokes, she could only be proud of him. For all the cheap snook-cocking contempt which became his stock-in-trade, her boy had turned out well, and journalists who beat their way past her well-scrubbed front door discovered that Mimi could be tolerant of, and even amused by, his antics. 'Every time John does something bad and gets his picture in the papers, he rings me up to smooth me over. A big present arrives every time he's been naughty' – one of them being his MBE, which he came and pinned to her breast, remarking that she deserved it more than he did. She displayed it on top of the television.

In 1965, when the fans pestering her outside Mendips had become an impossible nuisance, he bought her a bungalow in Sandbanks, an exclusive enclave of Poole Harbour in Dorset. 'I know it's stupid. But nothing could compensate for the pleasure he gave me as a boy,' she told Hunter Davies when he visited her there. 'He comes to see me as often as he can. He sat up on the roof for four days in the summer. I ran up and down getting drinks for him. He never shows much emotion. He finds it hard to say sorry. But one night he said that even if he didn't come down to see me every day, or every month, he always thought about me at some time every day, wherever he was. That meant a great deal to me.'

When he fell under the sway of Yoko Ono and based himself in New York, John would still phone Mimi every week for long conversations, during which they would tease each other affectionately. 'Hi, Father Christmas here,' was his customary greeting. She criticized his clothes, the way he flung money around and his mumbling incoherence, but she seems to have been unshocked by his increasingly bizarre behaviour. Even his stark-naked appearance alongside Yoko on the cover of their bonkers *Two Virgins* album didn't faze her; after all, she'd presumably seen everything he bared plenty of times before. 'It would have been all right, John, but you're both so ugly. Why don't you get somebody attractive on the cover if you've got to have someone completely naked?' He must have thought that funny.

In the 1970s, holed up in the Dakota Building in New York, he became increasingly eccentric and withdrawn. Unable to return to Britain for fear of losing his American visa, his nostalgia for Liverpool became sentimental and intense, and his Scouse accent (a source of embarrassment to Mimi, who had brought him up to speak an unaccented Queen's English) more marked. He asked Mimi to send him mementos – glass and china, a grandfather clock, old postcards and photographs – remembered from Mendips. He even started to wear his old

Quarry Bank school tie and urged Mimi to come and live in an apartment in the Dakota. Her work being done, her bones weary, she pooh-poohed the idea: 'No fear, John. You'll never catch me over there. I have never liked Americans. And you shouldn't be there either, it's no good for you.'

It wasn't. One morning in December 1980, two months after John's fortieth birthday, Mimi was lying in bed and heard his name mentioned when she switched on the radio. Being drowsy, she did not register the context, and only later, when a friend of John's called by, did she hear the terrible news that her boy had been shot dead in the street by a lunatic. Stunned with grief, she cut off her hair. 'I will never recover,' she told the world in a statement.

In her final years, she moved back to Liverpool, dying in 1991 at the age of eighty-eight. Yoko Ono, Cynthia and her great-nephew Sean all came to the funeral. The Beatles have become a chapter in cultural history in which Aunt Mimi's mummy role is honoured, and Mendips is now owned by the National Trust, serving as an example of the civilization of post-war middle-class gentility that John Winston Lennon despised yet owed so much to.

Lucinda Stevens on her Aunt Joan

My father was banished to New Zealand by his stern Victorian father because he thought that my father's first wife was not quite the ticket. He bought him a farm and told him to get on with it, which he did. But as his parents had foreseen, the marriage was rotten and it came unstuck after the birth of three children, and then my father met my mother, who had been born in New Zealand. They married and had two daughters, my elder sister and myself.

New Zealand in the 1950s was a lovely place to grow up in, but the thing in those days was to get back to England. So in 1959, when I was fifteen, I arrived with my mother and my sister in London, where we were met by my aunt, who was my father's sister. She was sixty-one then. And it was just like looking at my father, whom I was very close to, and although we'd never met before, I instantly felt completely at home with her.

We went back to the Inner Temple and the wonderful flat which she had shared with her husband, a barrister called Conway Joseph Conway, until he'd died in 1951. After lunch, she asked what I'd like to do, and I said I had no idea, and she said, 'Oh, I think we'll wander over to the Tate.' So that first afternoon, we went to the Tate and there I saw pictures of my late uncle's family, the Wertheimers, who'd been painted by John Singer Sargent. Like so many German Jews, my uncle and his brother Bob had changed their surname, to Conway, also my uncle's first name. I thought, 'Crikey, how can I be connected to this?' But I was, if only by marriage.

Sargent also did a charcoal sketch of my aunt, which my uncle paid eighty guineas for. I was offered it recently by my half-sister's son for $100,000. A friend who knows about such things said they were being ridiculously greedy, so I didn't buy it. But I would love to have had it.

My aunt and uncle were childless, and I became the daughter she had never had. My mother and sister went back to New Zealand, and I was left there, in a wonderful boarding school which my aunt found, on the coast of Norfolk. I loved it. There was a marvellous headmistress called Muriel Kilvert, who was great-great whatever of the Kilvert who wrote the diaries. She had been a Wren and was frightfully jolly hockey sticks, but such a good egg.

For the first time in my life, I felt real security, both at school and with my aunt. I felt wrapped around with love and suddenly realized what a lot I hadn't had as a child. My aunt and I became very close, very quickly. She had so much to offer – I don't mean just materially, though that was part of it. There was music, there was art, there was history, there was a sort of conversation that was just so much more interesting than anything I'd known before. She was immensely well-read, a keen gardener and a superb pianist. She also taught me to cook, being a very good cook herself. At weekends she would say, 'You can do the lunch and I'll be your kitchen maid and

clear up after you,' and she taught me how to get things ready at the same time.

She expected a lot of me, in every way. I remember the first lunch party she had when I was with her, and she said, 'Now you mustn't gobble your food, you must finish at the same time as the person sitting next to you and you must keep the ball rolling conversationally. It doesn't really matter what you say, just keep going.' It was very daunting for a sixteen-year-old girl, but I coped because I knew she expected me to. And I enjoyed it a lot, especially at the end when she said, 'Well done.'

I left school when I was eighteen and then endured a ghastly finishing school in Paris. I wanted to go to art school, but my aunt was firm about this and told me that I ought to have some way of earning my living, so she sent me off to secretarial college. I know she was right, but I was pretty fed up about it and left with the lowest typing and shorthand speeds they'd ever recorded.

I used to go home for lunch sour-faced, and it reached the stage where she thought of giving me money so that I could eat out and she wouldn't have to look at me. Then I started working as a secretary, met my husband and got married. But it was very dodgy from the beginning and we didn't have any money, so my aunt did up one of the gardener's cottages in the grounds of her house at Turville Heath, near Henley-on-Thames, and we moved in there.

She was very fond of my husband. She could see that the marriage wasn't working, but she also appreciated that he was an attractive and charming man. We had two daughters, and she absolutely adored them and treated them like her grandchildren. I remember she came to fetch me after I'd had the first baby and I had the baby in my arms in her car. I lit a cigarette, and she asked if she could have one too, and so there we were, both of us blowing smoke over the baby.

As I got closer to my aunt, my relationship with my mother became ever more distant. Throughout my life, she had made me feel uncomfortable, and now she is long dead, I feel very sad about this. But she was supremely difficult: terribly emotional, always bursting into tears to make me feel guilty. My aunt was so calm in comparison, with a gift for making people feel welcome and comfortable. One of her friends said to me: 'She's like the Bank of England and the Rock of Gibraltar rolled into one.'

Later in her life, when glaucoma set in, she gave up her flat in London because she couldn't drive and settled in Turville Heath. I'd moved up to Oxford and often went to see her – about twice a week. We spoke every day. She died in 1995, aged ninety-seven, and I still miss her so much. There's so much I would like to discuss with her. Last weekend I was with one of my daughters and her children and I had this pang of wishing that she'd been able to see them, because she would have adored them.

But she lives on through us. One is given values and standards by that generation. Whenever I'm up against it, I think, 'What would she have done?'

THE GARDENER
by Rudyard Kipling

Every one in the village knew that Helen Turrell did her duty by all her world, and by none more honourably than by her only brother's unfortunate child. The village knew, too, that George Turrell had tried his family severely since early youth, and were not surprised to be told that, after many fresh starts given and thrown away, he, an Inspector of Indian Police, had entangled himself with the daughter of a retired non-commissioned officer, and had died of a fall from a horse a few weeks before his child was born. Mercifully, George's father and mother were both dead, and though Helen, thirty-five and independent, might well have washed her hands of the whole disgraceful affair, she most nobly took charge, though she was, at the time, under threat of lung trouble which had driven her to the south of France. She arranged for the passage of the child and a nurse from Bombay, met them at Marseilles, nursed the baby through an attack of infantile dysentery due to the carelessness of the nurse, whom she had had to dismiss, and at last, thin and worn but triumphant, brought the boy late in the autumn, wholly restored, to her Hampshire home.

All these details were public property, for Helen was as open as the day, and held that scandals are only increased by hushing them up. She admitted that George had always been rather a black sheep, but things might have been much worse if the mother had insisted on her right to keep the boy. Luckily, it seemed that people of that class would do almost anything for money, and, as George had always turned to her in his scrapes, she felt herself justified – her friends agreed with her – in cutting the whole non-commissioned officer connection, and giving the child every advantage. A christening, by the Rector, under the name of Michael, was the first step. So far as she knew herself, she was not, she said, a child-lover, but, for all his faults, she had been very fond of George, and she pointed out that little Michael had his father's mouth to a line; which made something to build upon.

As a matter of fact, it was the Turrell forehead, broad, low, and well-shaped, with the widely spaced eyes beneath it, that Michael had most faithfully reproduced. His mouth was somewhat better cut than the family type. But Helen, who would concede nothing good to his mother's side, vowed he was a Turrell all over, and, there being no one to contradict, the likeness was established.

In a few years Michael took his place, as accepted as Helen had always been – fearless, philosophical, and fairly good-looking. At six, he wished to know why he could not call her 'Mummy', as other boys called their mothers. She explained that she was only his auntie, and that aunties were not quite the same as mummies, but that, if it gave him pleasure, he might call her 'Mummy' at bedtime, for a pet-name between themselves.

Michael kept his secret most loyally, but Helen, as usual, explained the fact to her friends; which when Michael heard, he raged.

'Why did you tell? *Why* did you tell?' came at the end of the storm.

'Because it's always best to tell the truth,' Helen answered, her arm round him as he shook in his cot.

'All right, but when the troof's ugly I don't think it's nice.'

'Don't you, dear?'

'No, I don't, and' – she felt the small body stiffen – 'now you've told, I won't call you "Mummy" any more – not even at bedtimes.'

'But isn't that rather unkind?' said Helen softly.

'I don't care! You've hurted me in my insides and I'll hurt you back. I'll hurt you as long as I live!'

'Don't, oh, don't talk like that, dear! You don't know what –'

'I will! And when I'm dead I'll hurt you worse!'

'Thank goodness, I shall be dead long before you, darling.'

'Huh! Emma says, "Never know your luck."' (Michael had been talking to Helen's elderly flat-faced maid.) 'Lots of little boys die quite soon. So'll I. *Then* you'll see!'

Helen caught her breath and moved towards the door, but the wail of 'Mummy! Mummy!' drew her back again, and the two wept together.

At ten years old, after two terms at a prep. school, something or somebody gave him the idea that his civil status was not quite regular. He attacked Helen on the subject, breaking down her stammered defences with the family directness.

'Don't believe a word of it,' he said, cheerily, at the end. 'People wouldn't have talked like they did if my people had been married. But don't you bother, Auntie. I've found out all about my sort in English Hist'ry and the Shakespeare bits. There was William the Conqueror to begin with, and – oh, heaps more, and they all got on first-rate. 'Twon't make any difference to you, my being that – will it?'

'As if anything could –' she began.

'All right. We won't talk about it any more if it makes you cry.' He never mentioned the thing again of his own will, but when, two years later, he skilfully managed to have measles in the holidays, as his temperature went up to the appointed one hundred and four he muttered of nothing else, till Helen's voice, piercing at last his delirium, reached him with assurance that nothing on earth or beyond could make any difference between them.

The terms at his public school and the wonderful Christmas, Easter, and Summer holidays followed each other, variegated and glorious as jewels on a string; and as jewels Helen treasured them. In due time Michael developed his own interests, which ran their courses and gave way to others; but his interest in Helen was constant and increasing throughout. She repaid it with all that she had of affection or could command of counsel and money; and since Michael was no fool, the War took him just before what was like to have been a most promising career.

He was to have gone up to Oxford, with a scholarship, in October. At the end of August he was on the edge of joining the first holocaust of public-school boys who threw themselves into the Line; but the captain of his O.T.C., where he had been sergeant for nearly a year, headed him off and steered him directly to a commission in a battalion so new that half of it still wore the old Army red, and the other half was breeding meningitis through living overcrowdedly in damp tents. Helen had been shocked at the idea of direct enlistment.

'But it's in the family,' Michael laughed.

'You don't mean to tell me that you believed that old story

all this time?' said Helen. (Emma, her maid, had been dead now several years.) 'I gave you my word of honour – and I give it again – that – that it's all right. It is indeed.'

'Oh, that doesn't worry me. It never did,' he replied valiantly. 'What I meant was, I should have got into the show earlier if I'd enlisted – like my grandfather.'

'Don't talk like that! Are you afraid of its ending so soon, then?'

'No such luck. You know what K says.'

'Yes. But my banker told me last Monday it couldn't possibly last beyond Christmas – for financial reasons.'

'Hope he's right, but our Colonel – and he's a Regular – says it's going to be a long job.'

Michael's battalion was fortunate in that, by some chance which meant several 'leaves', it was used for coast-defence among shallow trenches on the Norfolk coast; thence sent north to watch the mouth of a Scotch estuary, and, lastly, held for weeks on a baseless rumour of distant service. But, the very day that Michael was to have met Helen for four whole hours at a railway-junction up the line, it was hurled out, to help make good the wastage of Loos, and he had only just time to send her a wire of farewell.

In France luck again helped the battalion. It was put down near the Salient, where it led a meritorious and unexacting life, while the Somme was being manufactured; and enjoyed the peace of the Armentières and Laventie sectors when that battle began. Finding that it had sound views on protecting its own flanks and could dig, a prudent Commander stole it out of its own Division, under pretence of helping to lay telegraphs, and used it round Ypres at large.

A month later, just after Michael had written Helen that there was nothing special doing and therefore no need to worry, a shell-splinter dropping out of a wet dawn killed him at once. The next shell uprooted and laid down over the body what had been the foundation of a barn wall, so neatly that none but an expert would have guessed that anything unpleasant had happened.

By this time the village was old in experience of war, and, English fashion, had evolved a ritual to meet it. When the postmistress handed her seven-year-old daughter the official telegram to take to Miss Turrell, she observed to the Rector's gardener: 'It's Miss Helen's turn now.' He replied, thinking of his own son: 'Well, he's lasted longer than some.' The child herself came to the front-door weeping aloud, because Master Michael had often given her sweets. Helen, presently, found herself pulling down the house-blinds one after one with great care, and saying earnestly to each: 'Missing always means dead.' Then she took her place in the dreary procession that was impelled to go through an inevitable series of unprofitable emotions. The Rector, of course, preached hope and prophesied word, very soon, from a prison camp. Several friends, too, told her perfectly truthful tales, but always about other women, to whom, after months and months of silence, their missing had been miraculously restored. Other people urged her to communicate with infallible Secretaries of organizations who could communicate with benevolent neutrals, who could extract accurate information from the most secretive of Hun prison commandants. Helen did and wrote and signed everything that was suggested or put before her.

Once, on one of Michael's leaves, he had taken her over a munition factory, where she saw the progress of a shell from blank-iron to the all but finished article. It struck her at the time that the wretched thing was never left alone for a single second; and 'I'm being manufactured into a bereaved next of kin,' she told herself, as she prepared her documents.

In due course, when all the organizations had deeply or sincerely regretted their inability to trace, etc., something gave way within her and all sensation – save of thankfulness for the release – came to an end in blessed passivity. Michael had died and her world had stood still and she had been one with the full shock of that arrest. Now she was standing still and the world was going forward, but it did not concern her – in no way or relation did it touch her. She knew this by the ease with which she could slip Michael's name into talk and incline her head to the proper angle, at the proper murmur of sympathy.

In the blessed realization of that relief, the Armistice with all its bells broke over her and passed unheeded. At the end of another year she had overcome her physical loathing of the living and returned young, so that she could take them by the hand and almost sincerely wish them well. She had no interest in any aftermath, national or personal, of the war, but, moving at an immense distance, she sat on various relief committees and held strong views – she heard herself delivering them – about the site of the proposed village War Memorial.

Then there came to her, as next of kin, an official intimation, backed by a page of a letter to her in indelible pencil, a silver identity-disc, and a watch, to the effect that the body of Lieutenant Michael Turrell had been found, identified, and re-interred in Hagenzeele Third Military Cemetery – the letter of the row and the grave's number in that row duly given.

So Helen found herself moved on to another process of the manufacture – to a world full of exultant or broken relatives, now strong in the certainty that there was an altar upon earth where they might lay their love. These soon told her, and by means of time-tables made clear, how easy it was and how little it interfered with life's affairs to go and see one's grave.

'So different,' as the Rector's wife said, 'if he'd been killed in Mesopotamia, or even Gallipoli.'

The agony of being waked up to some sort of second life drove Helen across the Channel, where, in a new world of abbreviated titles, she learnt that Hagenzeele Third could be comfortably reached by an afternoon train which fitted in with the morning boat, and that there was a comfortable little hotel not three kilometres from Hagenzeele itself, where one could spend quite a comfortable night and see one's grave next morning. All this she had from a Central Authority who lived in a board and tar-paper shed on the skirts of a razed city full of whirling lime-dust and blown papers.

'By the way,' said he, 'you know your grave, of course?'

'Yes, thank you,' said Helen, and showed its row and number typed on Michael's own little typewriter. The officer would have checked it, out of one of his many books; but a large Lancashire woman thrust between them and bade him tell her where she might find her son, who had been corporal in the A.S.C. His proper name, she sobbed, was Anderson, but, coming of respectable folk, he had of course enlisted under the name of Smith; and had been killed at Dickiebush, in early 'Fifteen. She had not his number nor did she know which of his two Christian names he might have used with his alias; but her Cook's tourist ticket expired at the end of Easter week, and if by then she could not find her child she should go mad. Whereupon she fell forward on Helen's breast; but the officer's wife came out quickly from a little bedroom behind the office, and the three of them lifted the woman on to the cot.

'They are often like this,' said the officer's wife, loosening the tight bonnet-strings. 'Yesterday she said he'd been killed at Hooge. Are you sure you know your grave? It makes such a difference.'

'Yes, thank you,' said Helen, and hurried out before the woman on the bed should begin to lament again.

Tea in a crowded mauve and blue striped wooden structure, with a false front, carried her still further into the nightmare. She paid her bill beside a stolid, plain-featured Englishwoman, who, hearing her inquire about the train to Hagenzeele, volunteered to come with her.

'I'm going to Hagenzeele myself,' she explained. 'Not to Hagenzeele Third; mine is Sugar Factory, but they call it La Rosière now. It's just south of Hagenzeele Three. Have you got your room at the hotel there?'

'Oh yes, thank you. I've wired.'

'That's better. Sometimes the place is quite full, and at others there's hardly a soul. But they've put bathrooms into the old Lion d'Or – that's the hotel on the west side of Sugar Factory – and it draws off a lot of people, luckily.'

'It's all new to me. This is the first time I've been over.'

'Indeed! This is my ninth time since the Armistice. Not on my own account. *I* haven't lost any one, thank God – but, like every one else, I've a lot of friends at home who have. Coming over as often as I do, I find it helps them to have some one just look at the – the place and tell them about it afterwards. And one can take photos for them, too. I get quite a list of commissions to execute.' She laughed nervously and tapped her slung Kodak. 'There are two or three to see at Sugar Factory this time, and plenty of others in the cemeteries all about. My system is to save them up, and arrange them, you know. And when I've got enough commissions for one area to make it worth while, I pop over and execute them. It does comfort people.'

'I suppose so,' Helen answered, shivering as they entered the little train.

'Of course it does. (Isn't it lucky we've got window-seats?) It must do or they wouldn't ask one to do it, would they? I've a list of quite twelve or fifteen commissions here' – she tapped the Kodak again – 'I must sort them out tonight. Oh, I forgot to ask you. What's yours?'

'My nephew,' said Helen. 'But I was very fond of him.'

'Ah, yes! I sometimes wonder whether they know after death! What do you think?'

'Oh, I don't – I haven't dared to think much about that sort of thing,' said Helen, almost lifting her hands to keep her off.

'Perhaps that's better,' the woman answered. 'The sense of loss must be enough, I expect. Well, I won't worry you any more.'

Helen was grateful, but when they reached the hotel Mrs Scarsworth (they had exchanged names) insisted on dining at the same table with her, and after the meal, in the little, hideous salon full of low-voiced relatives, took Helen through her 'commissions' with biographies of the dead, where she happened to know them, and sketches of their next of kin. Helen endured till nearly half-past nine, ere she fled to her room.

Almost at once there was a knock at her door and Mrs Scarsworth entered; her hands, holding the dreadful list, clasped before her.

'Yes – yes – I know,' she began. 'You're sick of me, but I want to tell you something. You – you aren't married, are you? Then perhaps you won't . . . But it doesn't matter. I've got to tell some one. I can't go on any longer like this.'

'But please –' Mrs Scarsworth had backed against the shut door, and her mouth worked dryly.

'In a minute,' she said. 'You – you know about these graves of mine I was telling you about downstairs, just now! They really are commissions. At least several of them are.' Her eye wandered round the room. 'What extraordinary wall-papers they have in Belgium, don't you think? . . . Yes. I swear they are commissions. But there's one, d'you see, and – and he was more to me than anything else in the world. Do you understand?'

Helen nodded.

'More than any one else. And, of course, he oughtn't to have been. He ought to have been nothing to me. But he was. He is. That's why I do the commissions, you see. That's all.'

'But why do you tell me!' Helen asked desperately.

'Because I'm so tired of lying. Tired of lying – always lying – year in and year out. When I don't tell lies I've got to act 'em and I've got to think 'em, always. You don't know what that means. He was everything to me that he oughtn't to have been – the one real thing – the only thing that ever happened to me in all my life; and I've had to pretend he wasn't. I've had to watch every word I said, and think out what lie I'd tell next, for years and years!'

'How many years?' Helen asked.

'Six years and four months before, and two and three-quarters after. I've gone to him eight times, since. Tomorrow'll make the ninth, and – and I can't – I can't go to him again with nobody in the world knowing. I want to be honest with some one before I go. Do you understand? It doesn't matter about *me*. I was never truthful, even as a girl. But it isn't worthy of *him*. So I – I had to tell you. I can't keep it up any longer. Oh, I can't!'

She lifted her joined hands almost to the level of her mouth and brought them down sharply, still joined, to full arms' length below her waist. Helen reached forward, caught them, bowed her head over them, and murmured: 'Oh, my dear! My –' Mrs Scarsworth stepped back, her face all mottled.

'My God!' said she. 'Is that how you take it!'

Helen could not speak, and the woman went out; but it was a long while before Helen was able to sleep.

Next morning Mrs Scarsworth left early on her round of commissions, and Helen walked alone to Hagenzeele Third. The place was still in the making, and stood some five or six feet above the metalled road, which it flanked for hundreds of yards. Culverts across a deep ditch served for entrances through the unfinished boundary wall. She climbed a few wooden-faced earthen steps and then met the entire crowded level of the thing in one held breath. She did not know Hagenzeele Third counted twenty-one thousand dead already. All she saw was a merciless sea of black crosses, bearing little strips of stamped tin at all angles across their faces. She could distinguish no order or arrangement in their mass; nothing but a waist-high wilderness as of weeds stricken dead, rushing at her. She went forward, moved to the left and the right hopelessly, wondering by what guidance she should ever come to her own. A great distance away there was a line of whiteness. It proved to be a block of some two or three hundred graves whose headstones had already been set, whose flowers were planted out, and whose new-sown grass showed green. Here she could see clear-cut letters at the ends of the rows, and, referring to her slip, realized that it was not here she must look.

A man knelt behind a line of headstones – evidently a gardener, for he was firming a young plant in the soft earth. She went towards him, her paper in her hand. He rose at her approach and without prelude or salutation asked: 'Who are you looking for?'

'Lieutenant Michael Turrell – my nephew,' said Helen slowly and word for word, as she had many thousands of times in her life.

The man lifted his eyes and looked at her with infinite compassion before he turned from the fresh-sown grass toward the naked black crosses.

'Come with me,' he said, 'and I will show you where your son lies.'

When Helen left the Cemetery she turned for a last look. In the distance she saw the man bending over his young plants; and she went away, supposing him to be the gardener.

La plume de ma tante

(Al Hoffman and Dick Manning, 1959)

La plume de ma tante
Est sur le bureau de mon oncle
Le papier de mon oncle
Est sur le bureau de ma tante.

If you don't parlez-vous français
This will be Greek to you
If you can't figure out what
The words are all about
Just sing la la la la loo.

3

Literary Aunts

'My own darling child' is what Jane Austen called *Pride and Prejudice*. Women writers often bless their work with this biological existence, comparing the production of fiction to the painful ecstasy of parturition, and in many cases, the creating of lives through the written word provides a satisfying substitute for the impulse of maternity, the crucial difference being that once a novel has been published, it requires no further nurturing and must be left to find its own way in the world.

So the woman writer may be left with a space in her emotional life which aunthood can neatly fill. Her literary imagination should bless her with the sympathetic ability to enter into the minds of her nephews and nieces, to understand them as independent beings and not merely as extensions of their parents. She can also introduce them to her own inner storehouse of thoughts, fantasies and tales, making her a source of wonderment. These were gifts abundantly held by the childless Jane Austen and Virginia Woolf – both great novelists and exemplary aunts.

Family was Jane Austen's primary interest. (She might well have concurred with Margaret Thatcher's notorious assertion that 'there is no such thing as society. There are individual men and women, and there are families,' though not her belief that 'home is where you come to when you have nothing better to do'.) She remained with her parents – her mother outlived her by ten years – throughout her life, intimately affiliated to her seven siblings and their twenty-three offspring. They made that unfashionable thing, a functional family. In the words of Jane's biographer Claire Tomalin, the Austen children 'grew up tough, not given to self-pity and notable for their mutual affection and support'. There were tensions but no feuds, anxieties but no neuroses, and they were free of the intense introspection which made the Brontës so inept at forming outside attachments.

This warmth of feeling towards the family is reflected in Jane's novels. Perhaps 'tribal' is the best word to describe their sociology: they weave the threads of compatible dynasties into tapestries, excluding outright exogamy (the tall, dark stranger from nowhere holds no appeal) but accommodating cousins, step-parents and second wives. The important thing is to fit in somewhere, with someone else. Marriage doesn't represent an assertion of independence or escape from the status of child so much as an extension of loyalty, the grafting of a new branch on to an ever-growing tree.

Jane regarded her own aunthood with something like pride. When her niece Caroline became a very young aunt, she wrote to her: 'Now that you have become an Aunt, you are a person of some consequence & must excite great Interest whatever you do. I have always maintained the importance of aunts as much as possible, & I am sure of your doing the same now.' This wasn't an ironic joke: in several of her novels, the relationship between aunt and niece is shown as stronger, for both good and ill, than that between mother and daughter.

Yet none of Jane's own aunts was of any emotional significance to her. Her mother's sister Jane died when she was eight.

One of her father's sisters, Leonora, lived obscurely on charity somewhere and was never mentioned. Her father's other sister Philadelphia was a dubious character, the widow of a surgeon based in India and apparently the mistress of the celebrated Governor of Bengal, Warren Hastings. Although clearly a figure of great interest to the Austen household, she was known largely by letter and repute, as she went to live in France after the death of her husband, mixing in aristocratic circles.

It was Philadelphia's daughter Eliza who captured the young Jane's imagination, not her middle-aged aunt. Cousin Eliza, fourteen years Jane's senior, married Jean-François de Feuillide, a dashing captain in Marie Antoinette's dragoons. Gay, flirtatious and insouciant, Eliza adored balls, smart company and amateur theatricals – did Jane record her traits in the figure of Mary Crawford in *Mansfield Park*? – and on her visits to England, Jane was dazzled by her urbanity. In 1794, De Feuillide was guillotined; some twenty years later Eliza married one of Jane's brothers, the wayward charmer Henry.

Jane had another pseudo-aunt in Anne Lefroy, a close neighbour with a remarkable knowledge of English literature who encouraged Jane in her early writing. It was with Mrs Lefroy's shy and intelligent nephew Tom that Jane conducted a flirtation which might have turned into something more serious had he not been sent off to Lincoln's Inn to train for the bar. Two years later Mrs Lefroy was the conduit to another abortive romantic episode, when she introduced Jane to one Reverend Samuel Blackhall, a pompous if well-meaning Cambridge don who sounds rather like Mr Collins in *Pride and Prejudice*. Jane was amused but not interested.

The link between the families came later, when Anna,

daughter of Jane's eldest brother James, took it into her head to marry Mrs Lefroy's son Ben. Anna had long been motherless, and Jane felt a special auntly protectiveness towards her, not least because she showed literary leanings (of which more later). Despite her deep affection for Mrs Lefroy, Jane regarded the match sceptically: 'I believe he is sensible, certainly very religious, well-connected & with some Independence,' she admitted. But 'there is an unfortunate dissimilarity of taste between them in one respect which gives us some apprehensions, he hates company & she is very fond of it – this with some queerness of temper on his side & much unsteadiness on hers, is untoward.'

Such reservations were brushed aside, and in 1814 Anna duly became Mrs Benjamin Lefroy. The marriage proved happy, and no more was said about 'queerness' or 'unsteadiness'. Aunt Jane remained bracingly candid, however. Once she wrote to warn Anna about the little son of Ben's elder brother – 'a very fine boy, but terribly in want of Discipline. I hope he gets a wholesome thump or two, whenever it is necessary.' She was not one to be emptily sentimental.

One can assume that Jane issued similarly blunt comments on the aunt who gave the Austen family a lot of trouble, but because her sister Cassandra posthumously burnt all of her letters that contained indiscretions or potential offence, no evidence of these survives. Aunt Anne was Mrs Leigh-Perrot, snugly married to Jane's maternal uncle. She was rich, the heiress to estates in Barbados, and childless: the relatively penurious Austens lived in hope that if either of them died, they would inherit some of the fortune.

In 1799, when Jane was twenty-five, an extraordinary and

scandalous incident occurred. In Bath to take the waters, Mrs Leigh-Perrot patronized a haberdashery. Its dastardly proprietors decided to blackmail her by slipping a card of lace into a parcel of goods she had bought. Accosting her as she left the shop, they produced the lace from the parcel and accused her of shoplifting. When she failed to grease their palms in order to avoid embarrassment, the proprietors' scheme became more ambitious. They reported her to the magistrate, who was obliged to serve a charge of Grand Larceny. Because the lace was worth more than one shilling, this thoroughly respectable middle-aged lady suddenly faced the appalling prospect of hanging or deportation to Botany Bay.

Bail was refused, and she spent the ensuing seven months confined to a filthy little jail full, as she put it, of 'Vulgarity, dirt, noise, from morning till night.' Mrs Austen wrote offering to send Jane to provide companionship through this ordeal, but Mrs Leigh-Perrot nobly endured it alone. Her accusers continued to hope that her lawyer would avoid the mortification of a public trial by buying off the false witnesses they had briefed, but the Leigh-Perrots stayed resolute. This was a risk, not least because the laws of the time prevented Mrs Leigh-Perrot from speaking in her own defence, and the seven-hour trial proved a close-fought thing. But the jury's verdict of not guilty was greeted with great applause, leaving the Leigh-Perrots with a staggeringly large bill of £2,000 – the best lawyers coming no cheaper then than now.

A year after this fracas, Jane's father decided to move the family from Hampshire to Bath, where they lodged with the Leigh-Perrots before finding a house of their own. The drama over and calm restored, Jane could hardly bear it: her uncle was lame, her aunt 'deafer than ever' and their social circle similarly decrepit and tedious. Nevertheless, the rich relations had to be kept sweet, in expectation of substantial legacies. Forbearance, sadly, was in vain. In 1817, at the ripe old age of eighty-two, Mr Leigh-Perrot died, leaving all his property to his wife, with only £1,000 reverting to each of the Austen children after her demise. By this time, Mrs Austen was widowed and the family had suffered further financial reversals. Jane herself was mortally ill and the shock of disappointment sickened her further – 'a weak Body must excuse weak Nerves,' she told her brother. Months later, she died.

In these melancholy circumstances, Jane had nothing to leave her own nieces and nephews, but they had cause to remember her fondly: she had been a splendid aunt to all of them. Caroline later recalled how as 'a very little girl, I was always creeping up to her and following her whenever I could . . . she would tell us the most delightful stories chiefly of Fairyland, and her fairies all had characters of their own – the tale was invented, I am sure, at the moment, and was sometimes continued for 2 or 3 days, if occasion served.' Anna remembered the same magic: 'Aunt Jane was the general favorite with children, her ways with them being so playful & her long circumstantial stories so delightful! These were continued from time to time, & begged for of course at all possible or impossible occasions, woven, as she proceeded, out of nothing, but her own happy talent for invention.' With Fanny, she indulged in one of her great hobbies, domestic amateur dramatics, broadly comic in nature and not always as impeccably decorous in moral tone as the censorious attitude to the performance of *Lovers' Vows* in *Mansfield Park* might suggest.

Perhaps Jane's finest auntly hour came in 1808 when her brother Edward's wife died after her eleventh confinement and she took in her orphaned nephews, Edward, fourteen, and George, thirteen. She found them some black pantaloons, let them sob and played with them energetically – 'bilbocatch, at which George is indefatigable, spillikins, paper ships, riddles, conundrums, and cards, with watching the flow and ebb of the river, and now and then a stroll out'. Their sister Cassy was also taken in aged eight, when her mother died prematurely, and a charming nonsense letter to her survives: 'Ym raed Yssac, I hsiw uoy a yppah wen raey . . . Ruoy Etanoitceffa Tnua Enaj Netsua.'

When the time for tales of fairyland was over, she had even more to offer. Edward's daughters Lizzy, thirteen, and Marianne, twelve, were taken out on the town to see the highly unsuitable Don Juan play *The Libertine*. ('We left [him] in hell at half past eleven. We had Scaramouch and a ghost, and were delighted.') Perhaps this expedition compensated for the intense disappointment Marianne remembered feeling on another occasion, when her aunt was closeted in a bedroom with her elder sister Fanny, and she and Lizzy had heard 'peals of laughter through the door, and thought it very hard that we should be shut out from what was so delightful'. Was she reciting choice passages from *Pride and Prejudice*? Marianne left another vivid impression of the hilarity, exuberance and fantasy which made her aunt so enchanting: she 'would sit quietly working beside the fire in the library, saying nothing for a good while, and then would suddenly burst out laughing, jump up and run across the room to a table where pens and paper were lying, write something down and then come back to the fire and go on quietly working as before'.

Her eldest niece Fanny seems to have been the favourite; at
least, Jane described her as 'almost another sister' and 'could
not have supposed that a neice would ever have been so much
to me'. She was the daughter of her third brother Edward and
lost her mother when she was fourteen. Jane often stayed with
her, accompanying her on her charitable visits to the poor and
taking her to the dentist in London ('a disagreeable hour').

Most important were their long and 'very snug' talks. Mature and self-possessed yet anxious, Fanny suffered in love, embroiling herself at the age of twenty with the earnest, evangelical John Plumptre and then panicking when the moment for commitment loomed.

Jane became her agony aunt. Should she advance or retrench? 'As to there being any objection from his goodness,' she replied, 'I cannot admit *that*... Wisdom is better than Wit, & in the long run will certainly have the laugh on her side; & don't be frightened by the idea of his acting more strictly up to the precepts of the New Testament than others.' But pragmatism came before piety, and she went on to strike precisely the right note – neither hectoring nor cynical – by entreating her not to think of 'accepting him unless you really do like him. Anything is to be preferred or endured rather than marrying without Affection; and if his deficiencies of manner &c &c strike you more than all his good qualities . . . give him up at once.' Her own romantic life had been full of false starts and missed opportunities: did she wryly reflect, as Anne Elliot does in *Persuasion*, 'that like many other great moralists and preachers, she had been eloquent on a point in which her own conduct would ill bear examination'?

Mr Plumptre was duly seen off, and Jane and Fanny spent happy times together shopping and gossiping in London, where they stayed with another of Jane's brothers. In the evenings, Fanny played the harp for parties of neighbours, smiting the heart of one Charles Haden. A physician attached to the new Chelsea and Brompton Dispensary, he was incredibly handsome with impeccable manners and lively conversation – a catch, one might have thought.

Jane observed his amorous condition with glee, drily reporting the details of 'a wonderful nondescript creature on two legs, something between a Man & an Angel' to her sister Cassandra. Mr Haden also came to nothing, however, and it was briefly the turn of the even more eligible James Wildman, who had inherited the estate of Chilham Castle, next to Godmersham, Fanny's parental home in Kent. 'My dearest Fanny,' wrote Jane, now painfully ill and debilitated, in a letter which is one long, loving tease. 'You are the Paragon of all that is Silly & Sensible, common-place & eccentric, Sad & Lively, Provoking & Interesting. – Who can keep pace with the fluctuations of your Fancy, the Capprizios of your Taste, the Contradictions of your feelings? You are so odd! – & all the time so perfectly natural.'

As for Mr Wildman, he 'frightens me. He will have you – I see you at the altar.' No offence to Mr Wildman intended, but 'Oh! What a loss it will be when you are married. You are too agreeable in your single state, too agreeable as a Neice. I shall hate you when your delicious play of mind is all settled down into conjugal and maternal affections.' But within weeks, Mr Wildman was out and it was a question of one Mr Hammond. 'Single women have a dreadful propensity for being poor – which is one very strong argument in favour of Matrimony,' Aunt Jane resumed. 'Well, I shall say, as I have often said before, Do not be in a hurry; depend upon it, the right man will come at last; you will in the course of the next two or three years, meet with somebody more generally unexceptionable than anyone you have yet known, who will love you as warmly as ever He [who?] did, and who will so completely attach you, that you will feel you never really loved before.'

She was absolutely right, of course, but did not live to see

Fanny finally hitch herself to a morose widower, Sir Edward Knatchbull, to whom she bore nine children. In old age, she became a rigid Victorian, earning the wrath of all Janeites by writing to her sister in a surviving letter of 1869 'that it is very true that Aunt Jane from various circumstances was not so *refined* as she ought to have been from her talent, & if she had lived 50 years later she would have been in so many respects more suitable to *our* more refined tastes'. But then Jane's clever, cynical turn had made her alarming to the sections of the family for whom, as Anna Lefroy put it, 'a little talent went a long way', the earnest, docile Cassandra being far more acceptable.

With Anna, her eldest brother James's first daughter, Jane had another sort of relationship. She was more bright and beautiful than Fanny, but more highly strung and a handful too. (It is significant that among the heroines of her aunt's novels, Anna loved Emma and 'could not bear' Fanny Price, whereas Fanny's preferences were the opposite.) Anna wanted to write fiction, and rather than consulting her aunt on matters of the heart, she wanted help with her pen. That is what she got, in letters which provide a fascinating insight into Jane Austen's own technique and taste.

Although she doesn't mince her views, she pays Anna the great compliment of taking her efforts seriously, as one practitioner, if not professional, to another. 'We have been very much amused by your 3 books, but I have a good many criticisms to make – more than you will like,' she begins one letter. She complains on the grounds of mimesis and verisimilitude – things which were simply not like life – inconsistency – 'she seems to have changed her character' – and dislikes excessive descrip-

tions – 'you give too many particulars of right and left'. A revelation about the past of another figure, St Julian, 'was quite a
surprise to me; You had not very long known it yourself I suspect – but I have no objection to make to the circumstance – it
is very well told – & his having been in love with the Aunt,
gives Cecilia an additional interest with him. I like the Idea: a
very proper compliment to an Aunt! – I rather imagine indeed
that Neices are seldom chosen but in compliment to some
Aunt or other. I daresay Ben [Anna's husband] was in love
with me, & wd never have thought of *you* if he had not supposed me dead of a scarlet fever.'

Anna did not prosper. Ben died young, leaving her with
seven children, and they sank ever further into genteel poverty.
Her literary aspirations fizzled out, though she published a
short novel and two children's books, as well as making an
aborted attempt to complete her aunt's unfinished comic mas-
terpiece *Sanditon*.

Jane must at some level have regarded her novels as her con-
tribution to this family tree of births, deaths and marriages. 'As
I very much wish to see your Jemima,' she wrote to Anna after
the birth of her first child, 'I am sure you will like to see my
Emma & have therefore great pleasure in sending it for your
perusal.' *Emma* was another of her own darling children:
would it also be fanciful to see the lineaments of her beloved
nieces Fanny and Anna in its eponymous motherless heroine,
'the Paragon of all that is Silly & Sensible, common-place &
eccentric, Sad & Lively, Provoking & Interesting', a girl of
charm and imagination whose blunders stem from sheer adolescent wilfulness and imperfect knowledge of her self? Emma
could certainly do with an aunt to steady her, and perhaps that

is the role assumed by her loving and sympathetic but candid and clear-eyed narrator.

Elizabeth Bennet in *Pride and Prejudice* needs no such careful handling. Mature beyond her years, she is robust in her values and attitudes to the point of pertness. Her problem is her parents – a stupid, shallow mother with hysterical tendencies; a cynical, cowardly father who avoids confrontation – and how best to get away from them. She needs to be treated like the adult that she is, and the only person who does so is her aunt Mrs Gardiner – not her blood aunt, interestingly, but the wife of Mrs Bennet's tradesman brother. She is 'an amiable, intelligent, elegant woman', neither smart nor sophisticated, but thoroughly respectable and possessed of that peculiarly Austenian virtue, 'candour' or plain speaking. In contrast to her quiet voice of middle-class reason booms the arrogance of Darcy's own monstrous aunt Lady Catherine de Bourgh. She is nothing more than a caricature of entitled nobbish hauteur, but her utterances have a comic vitality which leaves thoroughly decent Mrs Gardiner seeming merely pallid.

In Jane's next novel, *Mansfield Park*, aunts are much more subtly and effectively contrasted. Fanny Price's parents are even more feckless than the Bennets (their nurturing of a child as timidly polite and conscientious as Fanny never rings true), and Fanny is willingly handed over to the untender care of her mother's sisters, Aunt Bertram and Aunt Norris. Aunt Bertram is a masterly study in female passivity. She is not unkind to Fanny and feels something like affection for her, based on Fanny's willingness to fetch and carry and play cribbage. Fanny reciprocates with dog-like devotion, not least because Aunt Bertram's patronage protects her from the bullying of

Aunt Norris, herself a poor relation at Mansfield Park, sublimating her irritation at her status by lording it over an even poorer one.

The brusque ending to the novel has a fairy-tale quality: Aunt Norris gets her comeuppance, sent off to live in seclusion with the disgraced Maria, 'where their tempers became their mutual punishment', while the Cinderella figure of Fanny gets to marry her handsome (if pretty damned dull) prince Edmund and thereby becomes heir to the palace that is Mansfield Park. A final neat touch is the way that Fanny's younger sister Susan is brought on to take her place at Aunt Bertram's side ('the stationary niece – delighted to be so!') and actually proves rather better at fulfilling the role than Fanny had been.

In *Persuasion*, the heroine has herself become the aunt. Anne Elliott is motherless but has an 'auntie', not related by blood or marriage, in the elderly, reasonable Lady Russell (a portrait drawn from Jane Austen's friend Mrs Lefroy?), in whom she can confide. At twenty-nine, Anne is relatively old to be unmarried and she is resigned to her role of looking after her younger sister Mary's badly behaved children. This she is very good at ('You can always make little Charles do anything,' Mary complains, 'he always minds you at a word'), though it leads to the most graphic instance of physical contact between human beings that any of Jane Austen's novels register. Anne is nursing the sickly Charles when his two-year-old brother Walter leaps on to her back and clings indelibly to her neck until Captain Wentworth gently removes him – a gesture which bears a curious dream-like resonance, as though a deeper burden is being symbolically lifted from Anne's shoulders. Moments like these make *Persuasion*, the last novel that Jane completed, wistful in tone, as if the author is privately fantasizing that there is still time for one of those missed opportunities to recur and redeem her from maiden aunthood.

But that was her fate, and it seems appropriate that it was a nephew, James Edward, son of her eldest brother James, who should take the responsibility of writing her first biography. His portrait does her little justice, however. Published in 1870, it is varnished with a high Victorian glaze of piety, discretion and decorum which never suggests either the quick, boisterous, restless woman whose cynical intelligence sent shudders down the spines of the strait-laced, or the warm, funny, affectionate aunt who relished amateur dramatics, played catch with her nephews and loved hearing about her nieces' boyfriends.

The other notable aunt in the pantheon of English literature was also commemorated by her nephew. The first full biography of Virginia Woolf was written by Quentin Bell, younger son of her sister Vanessa. An affectionate and even respectful work, it is nevertheless essentially different in style and intention from that of James Edward Austen-Leigh's. Alongside Michael Holroyd's *Lytton Strachey* and Leon Edel's *Bloomsbury: A House of Lions*, it stands as part of the first wave of writing about the Bloomsbury group, aimed at charting a network of intellectual and sexual relationships defiant of the blood-linked kinship in which Jane Austen was anchored.

Yet Virginia Woolf's parental family wasn't dissimilar from Jane Austen's. Both were profoundly English, one might say, in their ethical tone and mental structure: two large, broad clans of the upper-middle class with a strong sense of social responsibility and a good sense of humour, articulate and literate in their philosophy, and neither extreme in their views nor extravagant in their behaviour. In some imaginary meeting place outside history, they might have got on perfectly well. What separates them are the revolutions of the nineteenth century: the loss of confidence in the Church of England, the transformations wreaked by the railway, a nation that had become a democracy and seat of an empire, and a series of social changes that repressed more than they liberated. All of which made growing up female a far more complex and perilous business for Virginia Woolf than it had been for the robust Jane Austen.

Virginia Stephen was born in 1882, the daughter of the industrious man of letters Sir Leslie Stephen and his wife Julia. Both of them had been previously married, and the existence of children from these first unions made the dynamics of the cramped household extremely delicate: Leslie Stephen's daughter by Minny Thackeray was autistic, and Virginia was sexually molested by Julia's sons George and Gerald Duckworth. When Virginia was thirteen, her sad, beautiful and aloof mother died, and her half-sister Stella briefly assumed the maternal role before she herself died two years later. The tall, dark, narrow house they all inhabited in Hyde Park Gate, dominated by the presence of their morbidly work-obsessed paterfamilias, only added to the pall of deathliness.

Three aunts influenced this troubled, intense childhood. Virginia never knew her mother's aunt, the pioneering photographer Julia Margaret Cameron, who died three years before she was born, but the family maintained vivid memories of the open-door Bohemian lifestyle she pursued – a precursor to the easy sociability of Bloomsbury, it has been suggested. On the

Stephen side were two aunts whose characters struck Virginia forcibly. Caroline Emelia was a fervent Quaker spinster and neurotic invalid who followed the gospel according to Florence Nightingale and devoted herself to charitable works. For Virginia, the fascination was her vivid talk, full of stories and moral examples. 'All her life she has been listening to inner voices, and talking with spirits,' wrote Virginia, 'she is a kind of modern prophetess.' (After she died, Virginia wrote a memoir of Caroline Emelia; unfortunately it does not survive.) Anny, sister to Leslie Stephen's first wife, was a more vivacious personality, eccentric and absent-minded, who wrote about her literary forebears (she was Thackeray's daughter and had known Charlotte Brontë and George Sand) with an unbuttoned, idiosyncratic charm. All of them influenced the burgeoning consciousness of Virginia Stephen, that complex brew of dazzling genius and murky neurosis, intellectual clarity and emotional confusion.

In adulthood, she would mock quaint relics like Caroline Emelia as part of her rebellion against the Victorian tyranny of the family and the ethos which allowed a woman little choice in the matter of human relationships. She became openly defiant of her caste and its norms. For her husband she took an assimilated Jew, Leonard Woolf, in what soon became a sexless but loving partnership. Such libido as she had was channelled towards other women and the forbidden realm of sapphism. Fits of depression which sank into madness further intensified her alienation.

No wonder, then, that her fiction is rooted in a sense of human isolation. Jane Austen's novels always gravitate towards a consolidation of the bonds between families – a strengthening of the clan – but Virginia Woolf's create characters who seem to float around in the ether of their own thoughts, touching each other but never truly meeting or wholly communicating. Some of these figures may embody traits of her relations – Aunt Anny Ritchie feeds into the dippy Mrs Harbery in *Night and Day*, Mrs Swithin in *Between the Acts* bears traces of the brooding Caroline Emelia – but they are dissociated from the familial web that governs *Emma* or *Mansfield Park,* and it is their 'moments of being', their flashes of revelation, which validate them. Even in *To the Lighthouse*, where memories of her parents are revisited and their ghosts addressed, Virginia Woolf explores what separates people, not what unites them: Mrs Ramsay, an image of her prematurely lost mother, sits at the dinner table with 'a sense of being past everything, through everything, out of everything . . . as if there was an eddy – there – and one could be in it, or one could be out of it, and she was out of it'. She was 'alone in the presence of her old antagonist, life'.

Yet Virginia always felt the potency of family, focusing her positive affections on her elder sister Vanessa, a painter with a rollicking Bohemian existence based in Charleston, a farmhouse on the Sussex Downs, where she was variously accompanied by her three children, an estranged husband (father to two of them) and an otherwise homosexual lover (father to the third). She and Virginia were locked into what Virginia described as a 'close conspiracy', sometimes tetchy but always intimate and devotedly loyal. Virginia idolized, or at least romanticized, her big sister – Vanessa in her eyes being the maturely stable and sensible Stephen, emotionally undemonstrative, secure in herself as a mother and lover, fertile in her womb and easily productive as an artist. That she was in reality often horribly strained and anxious was something that Virginia preferred not to notice.

In this blind adoration there was inevitably a sprinkling of sibling rivalry too. It could even seep into envy, as when Virginia reflected only half-jokingly in her diary after looking at Vanessa's paintings that 'You have the children, & the fame by rights belongs to me.' Which would she have preferred? Although it may be hard to imagine the lean, acidulous and generally neurasthenic Virginia as a doting, domesticated parent, she did periodically nurse regrets about her childlessness. However, by the time she was in her mid-forties, past the age at which she could reasonably have hoped to conceive, aunthood was happily providing her with a compensatory emotional satisfaction. 'I scarcely want children of my own now,' she wrote in 1927. 'The insatiable desire to write something before I die, this ravaging sense of the shortness & feverishness of life, make me cling, like a man on a rock, to my one anchor. I don't like the physicalness of having children . . .'

With that element removed, Vanessa's offspring Julian, Quentin and Angelica could become 'an immense source of pleasure' to Virginia. She hadn't much liked them as babies, partly because they consumed so much of Vanessa's precious attention, but as soon as they became characters, she adored them. Reared with twentieth-century freedoms that she had been denied, precociously relating to adults as their equals, they were 'terrifyingly sophisticated . . . they have grown up without any opposition: nothing to twist or stunt. Hence they have reached stages at 16 or 17 which I reached only at 26 or 27.' The distance between generations collapsed – 'I can't believe that they're not my younger brothers,' she remarked of Julian and Quentin. 'It is very exciting the extreme potency of your Brats,' she told Vanessa. 'They might have been nincompoops – instead of bubbling and boiling and frizzling like so many pans of sausage on the fire.' As their 'poor dear dotty old aunt V' (a role she played up to the hilt), she would turn up the heat and gently cook them.

The most complex relationship was with Julian, the eldest. A big, clumsy and forceful lad, he grew into 'a vast fat powerful sweet tempered engaging young man into whose arms I let myself fall, half sister, half mother & half (but arithmetic denies this) the mocking stirring contemporary friend'. She charted the subtle changes in their relationship with fascination ('Julian . . . is very queer; one finds him noticing and feeling, and taking up what last year was imperceptible to him'), but their bond was muddied by his literary bent, an invasion of her pitch which made her uncomfortable. His first book of poems was published while he was still an undergraduate at Cambridge, and she was obscurely relieved at the tepid reception with which it was met. Later she wrote to him: 'I don't see why you should worry yourself to write a novel. It's such a long gradual cold handed business. What I wish is that you'd invent some medium that's half poetry half play half novel . . . I don't see why with your odd assortment of gifts – philosophy, poetry, politics and some human interest, you shouldn't be the one to do it.'

The undercurrent of disdain rose to the surface when Julian subsequently sent her an essay he had written on the art critic Roger Fry, in the hope that she might take it on for The Hogarth Press, the imprint that she and Leonard owned and managed. The risk misfired. Quite crisply, she rejected it:

'You've not mastered the colloquial style . . . so that it seemed to me . . . to be discursive, loose knit and uneasy in its familiarities and conventions.' Julian was deeply wounded, and a froideur descended. Months later, she apologized, claiming a befuddled head. 'I certainly didn't mean to say anything that could possibly hurt you . . . Don't for God's sake let us quarrel about writing.'

Quentin was more bumptious, less prickly – a plump, uproarious, good-time boy. At sixteen, so Virginia told Vanessa, 'he came to lunch. That boy really is a marvel. He drank two full tumblers of strong Spanish wine, where I can only take a wine-glass; and it was a hot day; and then he went off to shop, and seemed quite as steady as usual, and came back to tea, and had a long argument with me about poetry and painting.' Their conversation was knockabout, yet intimate. 'Oh to be Quentin and going to Rome!' she wrote to him when he was twenty and off on his travels. 'But my dear child, do you know that in half a century there will be methods of circumventing these divisions of aunt and nephew. By attaching a small valve to something like a leech to the back of your neck, I shall tap all your sensations.' (She was prescient of the mobile phone.)

Three years later, when tuberculosis confined him to a sanatorium, she kept him buoyant with gossipy, malicious and amusing letters, full of risqué jokes about virgins and queers. Over Julian's hot literary ambitions she sprinkled cold water; Quentin's, on the other hand, she fostered, pleading with him to give up the brush for the pen – 'Think how many things are impossible in paint: giving pain to the Keynes', making fun of one's aunts, telling libidinous stories, making mischief.' Eventually, he would take her advice.

The ravishingly beautiful Angelica, the youngest of the three and the child of Vanessa's liaison with the homosexual Duncan Grant, was Virginia's Pixie or Pixerina. She cooed and fussed over her niece, pulling her into a secret fairy-tale world of elves and 'witcherinas', as well as making embarrassing demands for kisses. 'She is sensitive,' Virginia observed, 'minds being laughed at (as I do).' She certainly was: in her memoirs, Angelica recalls her aunt's behaviour as more agonizing than entrancing. Her mother was generally withdrawn and said little; Virginia's petting was by contrast overwhelming, her manner 'ingratiating, even abject, like some small animal trying to take what it knows is forbidden'.

Yet there is no doubt that the children were as mesmerized by their strange aunt as she was by them. Aunt Ginny may have been 'barmy' and 'cracked', but she certainly wasn't boring. The temperature rose when she came into the picture, and the three of them loved to exchange reports of the latest volleys from her loose cannon. 'I saw Virginia for a moment,' wrote Julian, 'she only had time for one story and a mere handful of vicious remarks and to betray one important secret.'

Then came tragedy, in what was perhaps the most shocking of all the premature deaths in Virginia Woolf's history. In March 1937, notwithstanding his family's pleas, Julian volunteered as an ambulance driver for the Republican cause in the Spanish Civil War. Four months later, he was killed, aged twenty-nine, by a shell. Everyone had known that the risk of such a catastrophe was high, but the family's response to the news was incredulous. Twelve days later, in an ache of melancholy and remorse, his stunned aunt very quickly wrote down 'what I remember about Julian':

[his] 'peculiar way of standing; his gestures were, as they say, characteristic. He made sharp quick movements, very sudden, considering how large and big he was, & oddly graceful. I remember his intent expression; seriously look-ing, I suppose at toast or eggs, through his spectacles . . .

[the last time she saw him, sitting at the wheel of a car] 'frowning, looking very magnificent, in his shirt sleeves; with an expression as if he had made up his mind & were determined, though there was this obstacle – the car wouldn't start. Then suddenly it jerked off"; [his] 'rather caustic teasing. He thought I wanted to give pain. He thought me cruel, as Clive [Julian's father] thinks me; but he told me . . . that he never doubted the warmth of my feelings; that I suffered a great deal: that I had very strong affections . . .

[the 'damned literary question', over which she is painfully honest] 'I was always critical of his writing, partly I suspect from the usual generation jealousy; partly from my own enviousness of anyone who can do in writing what I can't do. . . . 'I thought him "very careless", not an artist, too personal in what he wrote, & "all over the place". This is the one thing I regret in our relationship: that I might have encouraged him more as a writer.'

Most poignant and vivid of all is the painting of a little scene when the decision to leave for Spain was still unmade. 'I want-ed him to stay. And then again I felt, he's afraid I shall try to persuade him not to go. So all I said was, Look here Julian, if you ever want a meal, you've only to ring us up. Yes he said rather doubtingly, as if we might be too busy. So I insisted. We

can't see too much of you. And followed him into the hall, &
put my arm round him & said You can't think how nice it is
having you back [from China, where he had spent some time
teaching]. & we half kissed; & he looked pleased & said Do
you feel that? And I said yes, & it was as if he asked me to forgive him for all the worry; and then off he stumped in his great
hat and thick coat.'

A mother could have followed him; an aunt is left at the
door, only half kissed.

I Have an Aunt Eliza

(from the film *Sunshine Suzie*, 1931)

I have an Aunt Eliza,
As wealthy as can be,
I act as her adviser,
And she believes in me.
I love my Aunt Eliza,
We never disagree
She used to be a miser,
I taught her not to be.

To flatter her is wiser,
Although she's fat and old,
I'm glad she's an outsizer,
She's worth her weight in gold.
But Aunt is not immortal,
And one day at death's portal
Like everyone she'll have to stand.
I've grafted on a monkey gland
So when she talks of dying,
I'll tell her that she can't,
I did it so that she'll live on –
And I can live on Aunt.

4

Heroic aunts

In the course of the nineteenth century, the aunt seems to march into history, striding through society with a spring in her step, no longer confined to her ancillary role in the family. The female sphere was expanding. Middle-class women could begin to define themselves beyond wifedom, motherhood, spinsterhood and dutiful philanthropy, as the narrow range of professions available to them at the beginning of the century – the stage, literature, artistic crafts, infant teaching – expanded into science, medicine, adult education and even political agitation. Railways and steampower increased their mobility. George Sand made romantic passion if not respectable, then at least a possibility. By 1900, the great questions about women – where should they stand in relation to men, what role should they play, how far could they go? – urgently required answers.

In this process, the unmarried aunt became heroic. She could be her own woman rather than one defined by her relationship to the patriarchal family. She had her cause, her ideal, her crusade, her destiny. She had work to do, which took her out of the home and gave her dignity in the eyes of the world. Yet her aunthood bonded her with the young, rooting her in the soil of family and what Keats called 'the holiness of the heart's affections'. This gave her enough of human love; no man need set her fluttering, no batsqueak of erotic yearning seems to have troubled her existence.

Let us look at three examples of this noble breed. First, Caroline Herschel, whose auntliness was forged by her partnership with her brother. Born in Hanover in 1750, Caroline was the eighth child of an oboist in the foot guards. Her illiterate mother could not understand a girl aspiring to anything more than domestic chores, but her father was more encouraging. When he died in 1767, Caroline, aged seventeen, was left at the mercy of her mother, who reluctantly allowed her to apprentice herself to a dressmaker. But she aspired to higher things than that and eventually followed her adored elder brother William to Bath, where he had been appointed Organist and Director of Music in the Octagon Chapel. William primarily wanted Caroline as his housekeeper, but he also had the idea that she could be trained up as a professional singer.

It was tough at first. Caroline had little English and felt intimidated by the fashionable folk who milled around the town. Her brother was a hard taskmaster, giving her three singing lessons a day and expecting her to double up with arduous domestic duties, but she soon doggedly succeeded in establishing herself as soprano soloist in the Handel oratorios. But just as her reputation was blossoming, William was losing interest in music and becoming absorbed in astronomy. For this hobby he needed large telescopes that he built himself, assigning Caroline the exhausting job of polishing the lenses.

Gradually William's hobby became an obsession. All the hours of unclouded darkness were consumed in observations, and Caroline reported that in order to keep her brother 'alife [*sic*], I was even obliged to feed him by putting the vitals by bits into his mouth'. In 1781, by which time he had become expert, he discovered the planet Uranus and was in consequence rewarded with a pension from George III. A grace-and-favour cottage was granted him near Windsor Castle, and his duties included giving guided tours of the skies to the royal family.

So he abandoned music, and Caroline abandoned her promising singing career too, in order to record her brother's celestial observations, as well as run his daily life. For twenty years, the rigours were unending. Throughout every night that weather permitted, William would keep his eye to the telescope, calling out what he saw to Caroline, who sat at an adjacent table with a ledger, a clock and a copy of Flamsteed's atlas of the heavens. It was often dreary labour, but their efforts resulted in the charting of over two and a half thousand previously unknown nebulae. And to be fair to William, he insisted that his sister took her share of the honour. In the course of their great research, Caroline became a learned astronomer in her own right, discovering eight comets with the help of a telescope that William had built specially for her. Her revision of Flamsteed's by now quite outdated catalogue was published by the Royal Society in 1798, under her own name.

Caroline was granted her own royal pension, and high society began to lionize her. Far from dreary or solitary by temperament, she liked a bit of fun as well as the chance to get out, and she enjoyed these glamorous attentions: Fanny Burney described her as 'very little, very gentle, very modest and very ingenuous; her manners are those of a person unhackneyed and unawed by the world, yet desirous to meet and return its smiles'. But her inner life had become discombobulated when William, at the late age of forty-nine, decided to marry a widow. After decades of slavish admiration and loyalty, Caroline felt spurned and wounded and moved into lodgings when William and his new wife went to live in Slough. Fortunately, Mary Herschel proved a thoroughly good thing, and the tensions were happily resolved when she produced a son John, on whom Caroline instantly doted.

When William died in 1822, Caroline, now aged seventy-two, made a foolish decision to return to Hanover, where she believed she would soon end her days. But she lived on for another twenty-five years, and according to her first biographer, ' "Why did I leave happy England?" was often her cry.' Her thoroughly English nephew provided her consolation, the reason to keep living. John Herschel grew into an intellectually prodigious young man who read mathematics at Cambridge and associated himself with Charles Babbage's early experiments in computing, as well as investigating the fields of mechanics, electricity, optics, acoustics and photography. Caroline fondly recalled witnessing the early signs of his scientific bent:

> Many a half or whole holiday he was allowed to spend with me ... dedicated to making experiments in chemistry, where generally all boxes, tops of tea-canisters, pepperboxes, teacups &c served for the necessary vessels, and the sand-tub furnished the matter to be analysed. I only had to take care to exclude water, which would have produced havoc on my carpet.

There were so many paths that this brilliant youth could have taken, but before his death, his father persuaded him to continue the astronomical line, concentrating on the search for double stars. Caroline herself could no longer observe – her eyes were too old, and where she lived in Hanover 'at the heavens there is no getting for the high roofs of the opposite houses', but she still had the will and the energy to help. With astonishing self-sacrifice, she undertook at the age of seventy-five the massive task of reorganizing the catalogues of nebulae. This work was never published, but it won her the Gold Medal of the Astronomical Society.

Ironically, Caroline was forever urging her nephew to cool down and allow himself some of the ordinary life that she had been totally denied in the service of her brother:

I wish often that I could see what you were doing, that I might give you a caution (if necessary) not to overwork yourself like your dear father did . . . dear nephew, I beg you will consider your health. Encroach not too much on the hours which should be given to sleep. I know how wretched and feverish one feels after two or three nights waking, and I fear you have been too eager at your twenty-foot, and your telling me that you have been unwell for some months, and now only begin to feel better, makes me very unhappy . . . I should be very sorry on your account, for [*sic*] if I should not live long enough to know you comfortably married . . . if you can meet with a good-natured, handsome and sensible young lady, pray think of it, and do not wait till you are old and cross. And let me know in time that I may set hands to work to make the bridal robe; here are women who work exquisitely, and at a price within the reach of my purse.

At least she soon had her way on this last score, and thereafter lived for news of John, his wife and their children. Of her £100 annual pension, she devoted half to presents for them. 'You must give me leave to send you any publication you can think of,' she wrote in her tangled English, 'without mentioning anything about paying for them. For it is necessary I should every now and then lay out a little of my spare cash in that for the sake of supporting the reputation of being a learned lady (there is for you), for I am not only looked at for such a one but even stared at here in Hanover.'

John honourably protested. 'If you are bent on giving me something truly valuable – infinitely more so than money . . . if you want to give me what I shall really prize highly, let it be your portrait in oils of the size of my father's. Let me send back the money and employ part of it in engaging a good Hanoverian artist to paint it.'

In 1832, he took his wife and children to visit her in Hanover. She was eighty-one, he wrote,

> but wonderfully well and very nicely and comfortably
> lodged; and we have since been on the full trot. She runs
> about the town with me and skips up her two flights of
> stairs as light and fresh at least as some folks I could name
> who are not a fourth part of her age . . . in the morning till
> eleven or twelve she is dull and weary, but as the day
> advances she gains life, and is quite 'fresh and funny' at ten
> or eleven p.m., and sings old hymns, nay even dances to
> the great delight of all who see her.

A year later, he took his family off with a large telescope to the clear skies of the Cape of Good Hope. 'Ja! If I was thirty or forty years junger and could go too, in Gottes nahmen,' she wrote when she heard the news. They stayed in South Africa for four years, during which he gathered enormous amounts of fresh astronomical evidence and managed to maintain a lively correspondence with his ever-interested aunt. Eventually came the happy news that he was on his way back to Europe and would take a detour to see her. 'So now be sure, dear aunty, and keep yourself well and let us find you in your best looks and spirits.'

The reunion was not altogether a success. Aunt fussed over the diet of her delicate great-nephew. 'I rather suffered him to hunger than would let him eat anything hurtful,' she wrote, 'indeed I would not let him eat anything at all without his papa was present.' At 4 a.m. one morning, to avoid tearful farewells, John and his family upped and left without forewarning. Caroline was devastated. The departure, according to her biographer, was 'kindly intended, but it was a mistake that gave intense pain'.

But Caroline would not lie down and die. She continued to be active into her nineties, enjoying the theatre, concerts and opera. Honours unique to women at the time accrued to her; she was awarded honorary membership of the Royal Astronomical Society and the King of Prussia's Gold Medal for Science, presented to her by the great naturalist Alexander von Humboldt. In 1843, she sent John what he described as 'an admirable and truly interesting History of your own younger days . . . I began the reading of it last evening to all your grand-nephews and nieces who are old enough to understand it.' On her last birthday, aged ninety-seven, she entertained the Crown Prince and Princess of Prussia for two hours and even sang them one of her brother's songs.

Caroline Herschel's career illustrates the limits of possibility for European women in the period. She was someone of no inherited wealth or position who rose to celebrity without access to formal training or advanced educational institutions. Everything she learnt was imbibed from William, and her achievement was uncreative, unoriginal and entirely dependent on his activity. She was essentially a secretary, a drone, a handmaid. 'I did nothing for my brother but what a well-trained puppy dog would have done,' she admitted, and maybe she felt some bitterness about that.

For women of the next generation more doors were open and they could begin to act without being entirely beholden to men. Take the case of Anne Jemima Clough, born in 1822, the daughter of a cotton merchant and sister to the brilliant poet Arthur Hugh Clough, one of the golden boys of the early Victorian era who died young, his promise unfulfilled. As a young woman, she taught children, and in the 1850s ran a small school in the Lake District where girls were admitted, most unusually, up to the age of sixteen.

A legacy gave her some financial security, and she began to write and think about the problem of extending the education of women beyond the classroom. Among her proposals was a scheme for courses of lectures in higher academic subjects such as astronomy, to be given by eminent fellows of the universities. These proved such a huge success that she was invited by the reforming Cambridge philosopher Henry Sidgwick to take charge of a house in the town he had acquired to accommodate women attending lectures there. This was the seed of Newnham College, which opened in 1875 and paved the way for women's full membership of the university.

Despite opposition from diehard male dons and the scratchy jealousy of Girton College, founded two years earlier on slightly different principles, Newnham expanded rapidly, largely thanks to Anne Clough's fund-raising and irresistible management style. In 1884, her niece Blanche Athena Clough, daughter of the poet, came up to read Classics; four years later, Thena (as she was generally known) graduated to become her aunt's secretary. She continued in this post until Anne Clough's death in 1892, after which she became the college's bursar and wrote a memoir of her aunt, published in 1897.

Here things get a bit complicated. At first glance the book looks like a typical essay in polite Victorian biography, presenting a carefully edited picture of an endearingly eccentric old lady with magnificent white hair framing huge, dark, heavily lidded eyes. 'She was above all kind, with an inexhaustible interest in other human beings,' writes her niece, and she radiated 'wonderful goodness and sympathy'. Wisdom lay in her gaze, she had serenity, tenacity of purpose and a 'power of sustained effort in the face of discouragement'. She had no vein of asceticism and no tendency to proselytize: 'enjoy yourself' was one of her most characteristic phrases.

But read Thena's encomium a little closer and you begin to wonder. There is more than a whiff of the satirical backhander in the tone: for example, she had 'a great deal of the eternal child in her nature'; she suffered from 'an air of timidity and irresoluteness'.

> Miss Clough hardly ever met anyone in the passages or anywhere else without saying a word to them. This habit caused a student of another college to say irreverently that if Miss Clough met one of the students going upstairs, she said, 'My dear, are you going upstairs?' and if she met a student going downstairs, she said, 'My dear, are you going downstairs?' No doubt it often seemed a little futile and even tiresome.
>
> She was not learned and her way of talking was rather confused . . . she was wanting in the power of expression

and logical arrangement, and she had no gift for expound-
ing general principles . . . she undoubtedly suffered, and
was aware that she suffered, from the want of intellectual
discipline in youth.

She did not dress or walk well . . . [she was] curiously
wanting in artistic sense. She took pleasure in many pretty
things, and seldom, if ever, liked ugly ones; but she had no
perception of congruity in outward things, and in such
matters would be content with what seemed intolerable to
others.

What Thena actually felt was much more violent and neg-
ative, as one learns from the enraged, depressive diaries she
kept during these years, now part of the Clough-Shore Smith
collection in the British Library. 'I want to write all I think
and know about Aunt Annie,' she writes on the opening page
of a volume she started just after her aunt had died. 'I mean all
the piece of her that has been mixed in with me, perhaps I
mean all the piece of my experience that has been mixed in
with her . . . I know I don't feel the things everyone expects
me to feel.'

This was evidently a sensitive matter that festered at the roots
of Thena's being. She never set eyes on her father – he was
attempting to convalesce in Italy when she was born in England,
and he died in Florence only weeks later. His sister Annie then
elbowed her way in to help Thena's young bereaved mother
cope with both the baby and her infant brother and sister. She
continued to regard them proprietorially, personally conducting
much of their early schooling and taking them on holiday with
her. Thena, it seems, grew up both loving and resenting her

domineering yet ineffectual aunt, and her subsequent fixation could be psychoanalytically interpreted as the result of her regarding her aunt as a substitute for an absent father upon whom she vented a form of unresolved Oedipal anger.

Whatever the explanation, the miasma of self-lacerating remorse in Thena's diaries is as ugly as anything in the auntly annals. 'The nasty taste of one's own unworthiness is nastier than most things,' she moans, and there is indeed something shockingly horrible about a niece expressing so much venom on the figure of a barely deceased old aunt. 'I was as her dog,' she spits. 'Everyone says . . . such a loss to your life. But no one knows I suppose or realizes how I have chafed and champed . . . Mrs Sidgwick said she had always supposed it was for my aunt not the college that I stayed – I was taken aback, didn't know the answer. Why it was for myself of course.'

She had left home and her sweet-natured but retiring mother to find herself more freedom in what appeared to be the wider world of Newnham, only to find herself 'slavecompanionvalet' to a woman whom the world saw through a rosy glow. 'To most people she was a friend & sympathizer and helper in their difficulties or a very interesting attractive person whom it was a privilege to see & talk to.' But Thena, who dressed and undressed her every day, had to confront her 'incessant obstinate fussing' and 'fidgetting', her physical clumsiness, her inability to concentrate and her quick-tempered snappiness – 'I know I hadn't cried for years & she used to make me cry with her sharp little words.' Without being decisive or efficient, Aunt Annie could not leave well alone: she was a prize interferer, 'always so much interested in anything one told her that she made all one's plans for one'. Sometimes Thena would have to run off and smoke cigarettes in the fields to filter the stress. On one such stomp, she took a deep breath and told herself that her aunt's 'life was more valuable than mine, that to keep her alive was more worth doing than to develop myself, express my own soul'.

She tried to live by this epiphany. 'I told her I knew I was a troublesome self-willed niece, but I did always really want to do what she wished & she just laughed as she always did when things were getting nearly sentimental.' For all the kindness and sympathy she showed to Newnham girls, Aunt Annie was not deeply affectionate. Remarks such as 'I make you quite a drudge' or 'You'll be quite tired, taking care of your old aunt' or 'I like to be where you are, I'm used to you' were the nearest Thena came to receiving gratitude or even recognition that years of her life were being devoured in her aunt's service.

So why did she put up with it? Why did she allow her aunt to crush her? For an unmarried young woman to be trapped by the iron whims of an elderly relative was of course a common phenomenon of the Victorian era – fictional treatments include Aunt Stanbury and Dorothy in Trollope's *He Knew He Was Right* and Aunt Maud and Kate Croy in James's *The Wings of the Dove*. But this drama took place in a milieu in which women were emancipating themselves, and Thena was not without options: she was a highly intelligent and capable young woman who surely had the strength of character, as well as the social and educational status, to tell her aunt that she was going elsewhere.

Did she feel the need to make some sort of propitiatory offering to her dead father, or was her problem the paralysing lack of self-esteem that colours all her diary confessions? 'I have failed badly in all that I aimed at,' she writes. 'I know really that I am only a carcase bobbing about in the water – tossed hither and thither by circumstance.' The antagonism made her examine her conscience with a masochism that was almost Jesuitical in its solipsistic intensity. 'I always posed as an oppressed martyr ... doing jobs without cheerfulness & with a horrid duty-doing oppressed air . . . I am always thinking of myself & only think with an effort of other people. This is just the opposite of Annie.'

She set herself the hard task of untying this knot by writing her aunt's biography. It's a stiff book, but one which does its subject justice, and after publishing it Thena did at one level move on, finding personal consolation and fulfilment in the creation of the college's beautiful gardens. But she also remained cowering under her aunt's shadow, inasmuch as she stayed at Newnham for over thirty years after Annie's death, first as Treasurer, later as Vice-Principal. In 1911, the blues led her to decline the offer of her aunt's former position as Principal, and it was only in 1920, after a great deal of havering, that she finally accepted it, proving to be the outstandingly competent and clear-headed reformer that her aunt had never been.

Both Annie and Thena deserve great honour as founding mothers of university education for women, as well as for their aunt-like nurturing interest in the welfare of generations of Newnham students. The college today contains halls and memorials commemorating the name of Clough. One wonders how many of the undergraduates who walk past or through them make any mental distinction between aunt and niece – a small ultimate irony which would make Thena smile wryly.

*

Another late Victorian philanthropic spinster aunt who bequeathed her achievement to her niece was the remarkable Emma Cons. And like Annie Clough, Emma Cons was clothed in public-spiritedness rather than institutionalized religion. Born in 1838 into a family prominent in the music trade, she was influenced by the Christian Socialist movement and the ideas of Charles Kingsley, John Ruskin and Octavia Hill, all of whom were seeking to improve the lot of the poor by uplifting their culture and civilizing their environment.

After attempting to establish an all-female co-operative of watch engravers (on the Swiss model) and working in a stained-glass studio, Emma involved herself in all aspects of housing reform, campaigning for parks, playgrounds, crèches and clinics, as well as sanitary tenements. Her temperament was downright and bluff, and unlike so many other genteel lady do-gooders, she knew how things worked and how they were made and could therefore keep plumbers and tilers on their toes – one suspects that dithering Annie Clough would have infuriated her.

Her great cause, however, was temperance. Appalled by the link between alcohol and domestic violence among the working classes, she established a chain of 'coffee taverns' intended to provide conviviality without inebriation and in 1879 raised £3,000 to buy a lease on the Victoria Theatre in Waterloo. The area was in a dreadful state, infested with rookeries and brothels, and Miss Cons sought to make what she christened the Royal Victoria Coffee and Music Hall a beacon of moral regeneration, providing not only respectable light entertainment but also a programme of lectures and classes. The latter soon gravitated to a site over the road and became the foundation of Morley College, which still flourishes today.

Among the audience at the inaugural performance in the Old Vic, as it came to be affectionately known, was Miss Cons' six-year-old niece Lilian Baylis. A daughter of her sister, Lilian was a musical prodigy, but her aunt was more interested in her administrative skills, and from an early age she was seconded to help with little jobs and fund-raising events at the Vic. Then Lilian's family took off to South Africa, where they toured the townships and mining camps as a musical concert party known as the Gipsy Revellers, in which the little girl offered a curious *tour de force*: skipping while playing the banjo.

In 1897, at the age of twenty-three, her skipping days over, Lilian left her family and returned to London to help her aunt run the Old Vic. Despite royal patronage and the intelligentsia's admiration of an enlightened social experiment, the enterprise had not flourished. 'It must not be imagined that the movement to "elevate the masses" met with immediate success,' Lilian later recalled. 'On the contrary, the masses showed plainly enough that they did not wish to be elevated.' The attractions of low ticket prices and the good clean fun of ballad concerts, operatic excerpts, comic and conjuring turns, Shakespearean recitations, brass bands and demonstrations of scientific marvels simply could not compensate for the limited appeal of hot beverages and lemonade.

Lilian's starting salary at the Vic was £1 a week, and on this peanut wage she lived with and worked for her aunt for the next fifteen years. Unlike Thena Clough, she felt no resentment at this; in fact, she felt it to be her divine mission, and apart from Sunday morning at church (for she was much more pious than her aunt), she appears to have spent her entire waking life managing the building. This was no easy sedentary task, and she was often called upon to break up brawls, repel the incursions of criminal elements and brazen it out with the local council when it tried to close the theatre down for flagrantly breaching health and safety regulations.

Miraculously – and they used to say that she had God on the staff – Lilian steered the Old Vic through several almost terminal financial crises and somehow caused it to flourish. Although she successfully introduced cinematograph shows into the programme, her most far-reaching innovation was a gradual move away from variety towards the establishment of full-scale theatrical and operatic repertory companies. When Miss Cons was on her deathbed in 1912, she knew she was leaving her mission in safe hands. 'What about the Vic, Emmie?' Lilian asked. 'You are there, dear,' Emma replied, and then closed her eyes. Lilian scattered her aunt's ashes in a daffodil wood and hung a picture of her in the Old Vic's foyer, where her likeness was often taken for that of Shakespeare's mother.

After the First World War, the astonishing, ludicrous and magnificent Lilian Baylis continued her aunt's work, although financial exigencies forced her to abandon the principle of temperance. To the Old Vic she added another suburban London theatre, Sadler's Wells, and brought dance into the equation. Fat, blunt, myopic, slightly deformed about the mouth and possessed of a uniquely disagreeable speaking voice, this physically unprepossessing woman whose aesthetic sensibility was limited had unknowingly laid the foundations for three great twentieth-century British cultural institutions, now known as the National Theatre, English National Opera and the Royal Ballet.

Later in her life – she died in 1937, having become a legend in her lifetime – her nephew Robert returned from South Africa. Even though she more resembled some stalwart old carthorse, he called her Auntie Tiger. Sadly, according to her biographer, 'she was too bossy and formidable to win his affection'. Good nieces do not always make good aunts.

Caroline Herschel, Annie and Thena Clough, Emma Cons and Lilian Baylis were all exceptional women, making their influence felt in the broader social realm. But the Victorian and Edwardian eras were also rich in those who did humbler service within the family circle. 'Let not ambition mock their useful toil / Their homely joys, and destiny obscure,' as Gray's *Elegy* exhorts. The great majority of their stories remain unrecorded beyond personal memory. Novelists attempting to imagine their plight choose to emphasize their pathos rather than their heroism.

Trollope's *Miss Mackenzie*, for example, is the story of the difficulties facing an unmarried older woman of means living with her niece in a churchy village, where she fends off suitors after her money rather than her affection. Even more poignant is Patrick White's *The Aunt's Story*. Theodora Goodman is an unattractive Australian spinster described as 'at most, but also at least an aunt'. Overshadowed by her more attractive sister and doomed to look after her grumpy mother, she finds some consolation in her relationship with her sister's daughter. 'I am an aunt,' she says. 'I suppose there is at least that.' At least.

After her mother's death she makes a supreme effort to make something of her life. She travels to Europe but finds nothing there to fulfil her. She ends up in America, where she gets off a train in the middle of nowhere and wanders aimlessly until she is institutionalized. It is a gruesomely sentimental tale, which makes being an aunt seem like the worst of human fates.

Lack of a husband didn't stop most aunts cheerfully getting on with it. In the years before the First World War, the poet Stevie Smith was largely brought up by an aunt who came to run the household when Stevie's father ran away to sea. Stevie's mother was overwhelmed and Stevie herself sickly, but Aunt Maggie was, in Stevie's words, 'strong, happy, simple, shrewd, staunch, loving, upright and bossy', and sorted them both out. The opposite sex was something she regarded with disdain: 'Men!' she would exclaim disparagingly, as they proved yet again what fools they were. Her attitude to life was summed up by something she wrote in a birthday book – 'if you cannot do what you like, try to like what you do' – and on such a basis, her moral judgements were pretty infallible: Hitler, for instance, she wrote off at once as 'a very soppy man, a most soppy individual'.

There is no story to her life. Her pleasures were the perusal of the law reports in *The Times* and a visit to the local church, where she was wardrobe mistress for the boys' choir. Otherwise her days were filled with the domestic round and the quiet, firm, reciprocated love of her clever oddball niece, in whose writings she took auntly pride rather than intellectual interest. Stevie compared her to 'shining gold' and 'a lion with a spanking tail who will have no nonsense'. As Stevie's biographer Frances Spalding puts it, 'compared with her love for her aunt, all other intimate relationships in Stevie's life were abortive.'

As the Lion Aunt declined into dotage, the roles were reversed, and Stevie uncomplainingly fetched and cooked and carried for the bedridden old lady. She died after a stroke in 1968, at the age of ninety-six. In effect, this left her niece widowed. 'I know it is best really, because she would never have been happy ·or comfortable again,' Stevie wrote, 'but all the same, it is awful . . . I think in her mind I always remained the rather feeble child I was when she first came to take charge of us all. But I always told her – and how truthfully! – that I depended on her just as much as she did on me.'

KATHARINE WHITEHORN ON HER AUNT MARGARET

Margaret is my mother's younger sister: she's in the mezzanine generation between me and my mother, and my mother was always very maternal towards her. Margaret was born in 1913, and when my mother was about eleven, the family had a Swiss nursemaid who was trying to stop Margaret crying by bouncing her up and down. My mother said, 'You'll never get her to stop by doing that,' and the Swiss girl said, 'Well, you take her then,' and put her in my mother's arms. She was overjoyed, and from then on more or less brought her up – my grandmother being a minister's wife (Presbyterian) and constantly caught up in good works and committees. So in a way Margaret's relationship to my mother was more like mine to Margaret, and she's the nearest I have to a sister.

Margaret went to Cambridge in the 1930s, and that didn't strike anyone as odd because her aunts had been to university before the First World War. After graduating, she didn't know quite what to do, so she had a year in the US at Smith College, which she much enjoyed. Then she came back to Britain and became a teacher. My father told her not to, because if she became a teacher she would never marry, but I don't think she particularly wanted to marry anyway – not least because having children wouldn't have been physically possible. She had had a massive fibroid followed by a hysterectomy, and maybe in some way that liberated her into being the sort of person she really wanted to be.

My mother thought that Margaret had never been in love. I asked her the other day whether she'd ever fallen for anyone, and she said, 'Not enough to marry them.' But she had plenty of men interested in her early on, I think, and when she got to be a headmistress, there were lots of crusty old widowers proposing. But by then she couldn't think of anything worse. She was one of those spinsters who remained single as the result of a decision she never regretted to follow another sort of life.

But like Mr Chips, Margaret did have thousands of children – all of them girls. She was headmistress – a very, very good one – of Godolphin and Latymer, in Hammersmith. After she had retired, she went to stay in America with old pupils, and on her ninetieth birthday there was a massive celebratory lunch, where they said, 'You told us you didn't want any presents, so we passed a hat around instead and this is for your next holiday' – more than £700. And people from the school still come to consult her wisdom.

Her first job, at the beginning of the Second World War, was at a school called Mary Datchelor, then under a marvellous headmistress, Dame Dorothy Brock. They were evacuated to Wales, which Margaret loathed and still does. But she struck up there with another teacher, Nod Swithinbank – I ought to make it clear that they were not lesbians – and when they came back, they set up home together, first in a flat, then in a house in Hampstead Garden Suburb, and Margaret became headmistress of Skinner's in north London, in those days a school that was very Jewish in its make-up.

Sadly, Nod suffered from Parkinson's and they had the house adapted to cope, so when Margaret got the job at Godolphin and Latymer, they decided not to move. I asked Margaret how she coped with the horrendous twice-daily drive across London, and she said simply: 'By not thinking it will take less time than it does' – a remark which is typical of her good sense.

After Nod died, Margaret moved across the river, ultimately to Kew, where she had a flat in a house owned by her second mistress Vera Titmuss and her friend Beryl Viner, another headmistress. Until Vera and Beryl's deaths, the three of them lived together very happily. Now Margaret is on her own she's moved into an old people's home, but it's close to her friends and community, she has a lovely room which looks on to a quiet street and there's a garden and a cat, so she's really pretty happy in it. She does have her grumbles, but much less than most people of her age.

I think that she was a role model in more than one important way. A friend of mine once said: 'You're so lucky to have had Margaret, you always knew there was another option – everyone I or my mother knew thought you absolutely had to get married.' She demonstrated that the celibate life could be not just worthy and useful but joyous and fun; and I like to think that apart from the girls who may have been reassured by her example to try a life without a mate, there must have been others who avoided marrying the first unsuitable person who came along and found someone better.

She's always helped us with advice, and people tend to go to her with trouble. For example, when I heard that my husband had a tumour and wasn't going to make it, I didn't want anyone else to know, but I felt I had to talk to somebody – of course, it was Margaret. She has lent money to some, an ear to all of us; other people in the family have all been to her with marital problems or for advice about their recalcitrant children. She's wonderfully uncensorious, but she's got very strong standards when it comes to the way she thinks life ought to be. She always managed to defuse situations and help you to get less het up about them, but she was never soggily 'non-judgemental' where she thought there was right and wrong involved.

There were some things she'd done as a headmistress that she treasured, and one of them was the time that a girl asked to come and talk to her. After the interview was over, the girl said, 'Thank you so much, you've been so much help,' and Margaret knew that she hadn't really said anything at all – she'd just been a good listener, and that had unknotted the problem. Another thing she was proud of was an incident where Penguin Books had a display at the school, and some of the books went missing. Penguin wanted to brush the thing over, but Margaret wasn't having it. She rang the school bell, got them all into assembly and said, 'There comes a time when you've got to face up to what you owe to the community, and I am not having this in my school. Those responsible will put the books back and nothing more will be said or done if they are back within the hour. This is not to happen again.' And one little girl who had taken the books came and sobbed and gave herself up. Some people to whom I've told this anecdote say, well, of course, it worked because she said she wouldn't punish them. But that wasn't why: it was because she wasn't prepared to let it happen. She was incredibly tolerant, but when the crunch came, she wouldn't put up with it.

She's been a wonderful great-aunt too. It's her birthday soon. I can't be around but my sons are talking about how they can manage to be there. One day she was in Scotland and I looked at the weather forecast and all of Britain was going to be fine, except for snow that was going to fall on that one bit of Scotland where she was staying. I said out loud, 'Get that snowflake off my aunt.' And my son said, 'Your aunt? I always thought she was my aunt.' My husband adored her too, and would always greet her in a Bertie Wooster way, saying, 'What ho, aged relative.' But I'm afraid she hasn't inspired me to be a good aunt. I hardly ever see my own nephews.

I had other aunts too. There was Kitty, my mother's and Margaret's elder sister, who was always rather sour about everything, and Beatrice, an aunt by marriage, who was very fierce and rigid. On my father's side there was Jeanie, who was very nice; Maisie, who I hardly ever saw; Con, who wore a wig; and poor Nora. Nora had a miserable life in Scotland, married to a man who was horribly mean, and they always appeared to be frightfully hard up – my mother remembered her chopping all the potatoes in two so that everyone could have a piece. When he died, she discovered he'd got thousands and thousands in the bank, so she took on a new lease of life and bought masses of long-playing records. Sadly, she soon went too deaf to hear them.

In Bertie Wooster's view, 'In this life it isn't the aunts that matter but the courage you bring to them.' I've been particularly lucky in mine – and I hope they didn't have to bring too much courage to me.

Sarmad Sehbai on his Aunt Shamoo

I belong to Kashmir, the land disputed between Pakistan and India. Kashmir is also very near to Sialkot, which is now in Pakistan. When partition took place in 1947, we migrated to Sialkot in the Punjab. They say Punjab is not a place but a psyche. The people are very gregarious and gutsy, full of life, humour and generosity. So we settled first in Sialkot and then in Lahore, where most of my family now is. We have large families. I have six aunts, born and raised at a time when women were not encouraged to educate themselves. Simple reading and writing was thought to be enough for them and they would be married off at fifteen or sixteen; my mother was married at fourteen.

Shamoo was the youngest sister of all. We lovingly call her Kala, which means auntie, and Shamoo, which is short for Shamima, meaning fragrance. There was not much age difference between my mother and her, so they were quite close to each other. Being the youngest, they had a naughty bone.

We don't socialize much outside of the clan, because our family is so big. Every day there are festivities going on; eating at someone's place – your place, my place – everyone has the same style of generosity. Treating twelve or twenty people unannounced, you can just go to their house and be entertained.

My earliest memories of Kala Shamoo are of her at weddings. She's a lovely singer; she sings folk wedding songs and dances in a beautiful manner, though dancing isn't very much approved of in our family. My aunt and mother would create their own theatre; one would put on a turban, acting as a man, and they would create a scene. There was this song called 'My Lover, Take Me Along in Your Beautiful Car'. I remember there was a real car there, and they performed their little song and danced round the car.

Kala Shamoo is very lively. She loves dancing, laughing and cooking, but she is very politically aware too. Her husband was pro-Russia, a communist. Although my auntie is not educated or an intellectual, she has an acute sense of national politics. She believed in the People's Party of Pakistan, founded by Zulfikar Ali Bhutto. Both my mother and she went on this movement for restoration of democracy in Lahore, protesting against General Zia-ul-Haq, the military ruler who had Bhutto hanged in 1979.

As the procession was tear-gassed, this intelligence man from the police in plain clothes, bald and respectable, came up to my mother and aunt. 'You are very nice ladies,' he said. 'There is tear gas and a baton charge – why don't you step aside, sit in my car, and I can take you to a safe place?' So the two sisters, mistaking him for a sympathizer, went and sat in the car. But this man took them to the jail: this apparent gentleman was, in fact, a cop. My aunt and mother gave him hell: 'You nude-headed bastard, a minute ago you were calling us sisters and now we have become criminals? You are a cheat! You are an agent of General Zia-ul-Haq!' The poor man didn't know how to react to their fury.

In prison, my mother and aunt started dancing and painting walls with anti-General Zia slogans and cartoons. They made the lives of the guards miserable by turning the whole affair into a picnic. When they were brought to the military court, the major in uniform asked my mother her name, and my mother replied, 'My name is Pakistan, you are putting Pak-istan on trial.' 'No, lady,' he went on. 'What is your name?' Again she repeats, 'Didn't you hear, it's Pakistan!' And when my aunt is questioned, she says, 'I am the judge.' The major says, 'What do you mean, you are the judge?' So she replied, 'I am here to judge you, the military, which has illegally taken over my country.' No surprise that, at the end of it, they were both sentenced to prison for a month or so.

My relationship with my aunt is very loving. Since I lost my mother, she reminds me of her, especially as they were so close to each other. Kala Shamoo's husband was an engineer. They used to move from one place to another, and when they finally settled in Lahore, there was a daily ritual of mother and Kala visiting each other's homes. When Kala's husband died recent-ly, I went to see her and she was sitting in the women's quarter – men and women don't normally sit side by side. I kissed her on the cheek. She was very calm and composed. Now I'm based in Islamabad and she's in Lahore, and whenever I'm in Lahore we usually meet at weddings, parties, funerals. There are no expectations, no compulsory meetings, but it's a ritual that whenever I'm in Lahore, somehow or other we will meet.

She has three sons and many nieces and nephews. She is very proud of anyone who excels in the family. Her own daughter-in-law is a painter, and she encourages her so much. Her paintings are all over the house. Kala is very much in tune with the times. Her youngest son, who's into pop music, has his own band, and she's very proud of him too.

My generation of our family has been very highly educated in big colleges, sometimes abroad. My first play was produced in Lahore, at a festival in Kinnaird College, a very missionary

English-speaking female college, run by mostly white British women. My aunt and mother don't know English at all, but it was my play and everyone knew about me. I was not out among the audience but behind the stage somewhere, not even expecting them, actually. They were accompanied by their nieces and daughters, who are all well educated, and they see these white women standing at the gates, and no one has the nerve to approach them. But my aunt and mother, clad in native shal-war kameez, confidently go up to them and say, 'My son's play, my nephew's play.' When they sat them in the front row, my aunt reprimanded the nieces: 'Why have we spent so much on your education and you can't even speak a word to the foreigners?'

Kala has very high standards. There are certain things that are dear to her: cleanliness, religion and politics. She's a very liberal person, not a mullah, but she combines belief in social-ism with Islamic teachings. Arguments in the family are nor-mally about the People's Party; she doesn't want to listen to anything against Bhutto or his family or the party. In her own way, she has seen poverty, misery and injustice, and being a patriotic sort of person, she asserted herself in politics. She thought there should be social justice in Pakistan; it was very bold of women in purdah to voice such feelings in the streets. She carries within her a whole civilizational experience – the folklore, the images of family structure, the familial pleasures, the liberating euphoria of dance and music. That sense of abandon has been a major defining influence on me and my writing. It is rare.

Except for my mother and my aunt, nobody else in my family ever got involved in politics. The other aunts are married to rather richer husbands and are ladies of leisure. My aunt has probably seen more of life than the others. The best thing about her is that she is not intimidated or impressed by any pretension, pomp, show or posturing. She comes across very simply, but she is not without substance and is never afraid of anything.

Our relationship does not change. If I met her at a wedding now, I'd just hug her and ask her, 'Could we have this dance?' She would probably say, 'My knees are not supporting me, I'm too fat for it.' And I would insist, and suddenly she would start dancing. I wish I could visit her more often, hug her more often, make her stand on her two feet and dance like that.

Auntie

(E. A. Searson, 1911)

At Goodwood on the Cup day, you will see her on
the lawn,
She's fond of sport and has been from the day that
she was born,
And some nasty observations have been made by
Father Vaughan
Re Auntie – poor Auntie.

She's simply great on horseback – all the fellows
tell her so,
Her habit is of course designed her gracefulness to
show.
Well, her habits are the talk of everyone in Rotten
Row.
Oh Auntie – dear Auntie
Auntie, Auntie, she's always right on top
She's a goer and she knows it, and doesn't mean to
stop.

5

Exotics and Eccentrics

Imperious and impetuous, yet brusquely kind and briskly sensible with her 'quick, bright eye', mobcap and gentleman's watch, Betsy Trotwood provides a template for the benignly eccentric Victorian aunt. A contented spinster leading a life of militant independence, she takes in her orphaned nephew David Copperfield when he runs away from London, sees off his persecutors, the ghastly Murdstone siblings, and then generously pays for his education and sets him up in the Law.

Dickens turns her into a mothering aunt. She rechristens David as Trotwood Copperfield, thereby implying her maternal claim. The softer emotions do not easily penetrate her defences, but what does crack through is sincere and heartfelt. 'You are my adopted child,' she tells David. 'Only be a loving child to me in my age, and bear with my whims and fancies.' David duly reciprocates with all love and respect, and the novel rewards her with a happy, active old age – we last see her 'fourscore years and more, but upright yet, and a steady walker of six miles at a stretch in winter'.

Dickens doesn't otherwise show much interest in aunts. His own played an insignificant role in his life, and the only other notable example of the breed in his writing is Mr F.'s Aunt, a minor if brilliantly vivid character in *Little Dorrit*, notable not for her auntliness but her psychotic alienation, manifested in a 'propensity to offer remarks in a deep warning voice which,

being totally uncalled for by anything said by anybody and traceable to no association of ideas, confounded and terrified the
mind'. With her incapacity to relate normally to her surroundings or companions, she is clearly the victim of a form of some
autistic disorder, and although her utterances have comic force,
she is no more than a bizarre one-off in the history of aunts.

But Betsy Trotwood has a large progeny. There are literally
hundreds of aunts in later nineteenth- and twentieth-century
English literature who share her characteristics of gruff, fearless good-eggery and staunch disdain of fashion and custom.
They may seem stern and unyielding on the surface, but they
only have to be scratched or tickled to soften. There's Aunt
Maybury in Anthony Trollope's *He Knew He Was Right*, for
example. A wealthy and rigid spinster, she takes in her niece
Dorothy and tries to match her with the repellent Revd Gib-
son. When this scheme fails, she adamantly and apparently
irrationally refuses to allow Dorothy to marry her heir, the
more agreeable Brooke Burgess, but eventually relents. Then
there's Mrs Touchett, Isabel Archer's aunt in Henry James's
The Portrait of a Lady. Living a peripatetic existence in amica-
ble separation from her banker husband, she is 'a person of
many oddities . . . who had her own way of doing all that she
did . . . the edges of her conduct were so very clear-cut that for
susceptible persons it sometimes had a knife-like effect'. In
important matters, however, she hits the nail on the head and
her opposition to Isabel's marriage to the sterile dilettante
Gilbert Osmond is based on sound moral precepts.

In the twentieth century, as women were allowed more freedom to roam, such aunts become increasingly wayward and
unaccountable. Published in 1956 and now established as a

modern classic, Rose Macaulay's *The Towers of Trebizond* contains the memorable figure of the adventurous widow Aunt
Dot, full name Dorothea ffoulkes-Corbett (and thought by
some to be based on Dorothy L. Sayers), who aims to convert
the Muslim Turks to Anglicanism. Together with her niece – or
is it nephew? the text is ambiguous – Laurie and a Turkish lady
doctor and the miracle-working Father Chantry-Pigg, Aunt
Dot sets off from Istanbul riding a camel. Her particular concern is the liberation of Turkish women. 'There is nothing in
the gospels about women behaving differently from men, either
in church or out of it,' she announces. 'So what a comfort to
these poor women to learn that they needn't.' But her refusal to
rein herself in gets her into endless trouble: at one point, she is
pelted with apples and tomatoes when she decides to take a dip
in the sea, 'while the women, wrapping their shawls over their
mouths, looked on in shocked stupefaction'. Towards the end
of the novel, she gives Laurie some splendid auntly advice:
'One mustn't lose sight of the hard core, which is, do this, do
that, love your friends and like your neighbours, be just, be
extravagantly generous, be honest, be tolerant, have compassion, use your wits and your imagination, understand the
world you live in and be on terms with it.'

The year before *The Towers of Trebizond* was published,
Edward Everett Tanner III, writing under the pseudonym of
Patrick Dennis, had enjoyed a huge success in the US with
Auntie Mame, a light and largely autobiographical novel based
on the author's experiences with his Aunt Marion. The novel
won further fame when it was turned into a play and film (both
starring Rosalind Russell), and then a musical (starring Angela
Lansbury on Broadway, Lucille Ball on film).

The narrator is a ten-year-old orphan, sent to New York from a respectable suburb of Chicago under the terms of his father's will, where his Auntie Mame, a rich Manhattan sophisticate, is to bring him up. The year is 1929; she receives the boy in her bedroom, 'wearing her bed jacket of pink ostrich feathers. She was reading Gide's *Les Faux-Monnayeurs* and smoking Melachrino cigarettes through a long amber holder.' As Aunt Dot taught Laurie religion, so Auntie Mame teaches Patrick worldliness: 'one day, July 14 1929,' he writes, 'featured such random terms as Bastille Day, Lesbian, Hotsy-Totsy Club, gang war, id, daiquiri – although I didn't spell it properly – relativity, free love, Oedipus complex – another one I misspelled – narcissistic, Biarritz, psychoneurotic, Schönberg and nymphomaniac.' To educate him further, she sends him to 'a school coeducational and completely revolutionary. All classes are held in the nude under ultra-violet ray.' The experiment doesn't last long.

Yet Auntie Mame isn't just a chic comic turn. 'That her amazing personality would attract me, just as it had seduced thousands of others, was a foregone conclusion . . . but that she should care for an insignificant, uninteresting boy of ten was a constant source of delight and mystification to me. Yet she did, and I always thought that for all of her popularity, her interests, her constant comings and goings, she was probably a little lonely too. Her critics have said that I was simply a new lump of clay for her to shape, stretch, mould and pummel to her heart's content, and although it is true that Auntie Mame could never resist meddling with other people's lives, she still had a staunch, undependable dependability. For both of us, it was love . . .'

Another late variant of the stereotype is Aunt Augusta, the central figure of *Travels with My Aunt*, a laboured novel by Graham Greene, published in 1969, which was also turned into a play and film (with Maggie Smith) – though not yet a musical, thank God. Its theme is in outline the same as that of *Auntie Mame*, but with a twist. A dreary bank clerk called Henry Pulling is visited by his long-lost aunt on the day of his mother's funeral. She decides that Henry needs the stuffing knocked out of him, so first she takes him on a smuggling trip to Istanbul on the Orient Express, then to South America, where Aunt Augusta pursues the love of her life, the nefarious Mr Visconti.

For Henry, the relationship is an education in the wilder shores of life. Augusta, who admits that she has worked extensively as a high-class prostitute, tells him that the woman he thought was his mother, Angelica, hadn't actually given birth to him but had merely covered up for someone, who hadn't wanted to marry the baby's father. On the book's penultimate page, Augusta's true relation to Henry is revealed: he calls her 'Aunt Augusta' and she doesn't respond; then he calls her 'Mother' and she does.

But without doubt the most vividly depicted aunts in the Trotwood tradition are P. G. Wodehouse's Dahlia and Agatha, who operate on the good aunt–bad aunt principle. Wodehouse was obsessed with aunts, partly because his own childhood had been so dominated by them. The son of a Hong Kong magistrate, he was sent back to England, like many colonials' children, at an early age and passed round his relatives during the school holidays. For years at a time he wouldn't see his parents at all. As temporary mother substitutes he variously endured Aunt Julie, who had three lovely daughters; Aunt

Nim, a portrait painter who lived in Bohemian Chelsea; Aunt Mary, a domestic tyrant of a literary bent, who lived with Aunt Loulie and Aunt Anne near Bath; Aunt Lydia; Aunt Edith; Aunt Constance and Aunt Alice, rectors' wives; Aunt Jane; and Aunt Amy. The psyches of Wodehouse's contemporaries Saki and Rudyard Kipling were deeply scarred by being farmed out in similar fashion. But Wodehouse adored school and must have been saved by his irrepressible tendency to see the funny side.

On the whole, he is anti-aunt. In the short story 'Jeeves Makes an Omelette', his alter ego Bertie Wooster describes his position on the subject:

> In these disturbed days in which we live, it has probably occurred to all thinking men that something drastic ought to be done about aunts. Speaking for myself, I have long felt that stones should be turned and avenues explored with a view to putting a stopper on the relatives in question. If someone were to come to me and say, 'Wooster, would you be interested in joining a society I am starting whose aim is the suppression of aunts or at least will see to it that they are kept on a short chain and not permitted to roam hither and thither at will, scattering desolation on all sides?' I would reply, 'Wilbraham,' if his name was Wilbraham, 'I am with you heart and soul. Put me down as a foundation member.'

Elsewhere aunts are blamed for all ills and failures. 'Behind every poor innocent blighter who is going down for the third time in the soup,' he moans, 'you will find, if you look carefully enough, the aunt who shoved him into it . . . If I had my life to live again, Jeeves, I would start it as an orphan without any aunts. Don't they put aunts in Turkey in sacks and drop them in the Bosphorus?' Bertie even dreams aunts: 'as far as the eye could reach I found myself gazing on a surging sea of aunts. There were tall aunts, short aunts, stout aunts, thin aunts and an aunt who was carrying on a conversation in a low voice to which nobody appeared to be paying the slightest attention.'

Agatha and Dahlia are sisters to Bertie's father. Agatha, according to Bertie in *The Mating Season*, 'is the one who chews broken bottles and kills rats with her teeth'. She has 'an eye like a man-eating fish' and 'wears barbed wire next to the skin'. Agatha reciprocates this low opinion, telling Bertie firmly that he is 'an idiot' and objecting to what she sees as Jeeves's malignly protective influence. Her aim is to pair her nephew off with Honoria, the fey and irritating daughter of her friend Lady Glossop. Bertie regards this scheme with dismay and adopts elaborately evasive tactics. But there is no avoiding Agatha's son, the young Thos, who comes to London requiring board and lodging and trips to the Old Vic. Fundamentally, Bertie is dead scared of his aunt: she is his superego, confronting him with his own inadequacy and superfluity. 'She made him feel as if he had omitted to shave and, in addition to that, had swallowed some drug which had caused him to swell unpleasantly, particularly about the hands and feet.'

Dahlia is something else. She is fond of Bertie in an exasperated way, greeting him with an affectionate 'Hello, ugly', to which he responds by calling her 'the old flesh and blood,' and in rare sentimental moments, 'my good and deserving aunt'. Formerly an enthusiastic hunter, she retains a brick-red complexion and formidable strength which in her prime allowed her to 'lift fellow-members of the Quorn and Pytchley out of their saddles with a single yip, though separated from them by two ploughed fields and a spinney'. When her passions are roused, 'strong men climb trees and pull them up after them', and at one point she knocks someone out with a cosh. She has another crucial virtue: that of respecting Jeeves and his knack for hauling Bertie out of scrapes.

The Aunt Agatha–Aunt Dahlia axis had long been the stuff of theatrical farce when Wodehouse created these two *monstres sacrés* in the 1930s. Plays about crotchety old maids who might leave their nieces and nephews some money but have rigid views as to who they should or shouldn't marry were common currency throughout the nineteenth century – James Robinson Planche's *My Great Aunt* (1831), Richard Brinsley Knowles's *The Maiden Aunt* (1845), Sir Charles Rockingham's *Aunt Hercules* (1867) and Lillie Davies's *Aunt Madge* (1898) all fall into this category. But the only two of these theatrical aunts who are remembered today appear in Brandon Thomas's *Charley's Aunt* (1892) and Oscar Wilde's *The Importance of Being Earnest* (1895).

Charley's Aunt is an astonishingly successful play which ran for four years following its London première, and according to *The Oxford Companion to the Theatre*, was once performed 'on the same day in 48 different theatres in 22 languages, including Afrikaans, Chinese, Esperanto, Gaelic, Russian and Zulu'. (Esperanto?) Charley is a Bertie Wooster sort of undergraduate at St Olde's College, Oxford, who is expecting a visit from Donna Lucia, his elderly widowed aunt just returned from Brazil, 'where the nuts come from'. Charley and his pal Jack are in love with two innocent young ladies but can't respectably entertain them in their rooms unless their guests are chaperoned. The chaps decide that Charley's aunt can serve that purpose and the girls are duly invited. To complete the party, they invite another asinine undergraduate, Lord Fancourt Babberly, known as Babbs, who can entertain the aunt, leaving Jack and Charley to spoon with the girls. Jack also invites his father, who is in financial embarrassment and could usefully marry Donna Lucia.

All these well-laid plans are thrown into disarray when Donna Lucia cancels at the last minute. Jack and Charley's desperate solution is to bully the reluctant Babbs into dragging up in the costume he was planning to use for the end-of-term revue and impersonating Donna Lucia. The comedy hots up as Jack's father starts an ardent courtship of Charley's aunt and the real Donna Lucia unexpectedly appears, accompanied by Ela, a young ward who turns out to be a girl that Babbs met on a boat and fell in love with. The farrago eventually resolves itself with the right number of appropriate marital pairings.

The same happens at the end of Wilde's *The Importance of Being Earnest*, a play of classical formal perfection. Here the aunt is called Augusta, otherwise known as Lady Bracknell, and she belongs to the *flâneurs* Algy Moncrieff and Jack Worthing. She must rank as the nastiest aunt in English literature, and subsidiarily she is one of the nastiest mothers as well. She represents a new mutation of the British aristocracy that has eliminated *noblesse oblige* and substituted ruthless self-interest: for all her hauteur, she is ironically the most vulgar character in the play, being shamelessly materialistic and cynical in her values and attitudes. Traditionally, even the starchiest aunts melt a little at the sight of young love, but Lady Bracknell has no atom of sentimentality and in the last seconds of the play can only accuse her nephew Jack of 'signs of triviality' when he throws his arms around his beloved Gwendolen and cries, 'At last!'

Was it the success of these two plays that fired a new vogue for comedies about aunts in the early twentieth century? The British Library catalogue records at least fifty from this era, many of them designed for amateur performance. Although they continue to focus on the themes of inherited money and a suitable marriage partner for a niece or nephew, they follow other plot lines as well.

There is the aunt who sloughs off her grumpy and frumpy carapace and becomes a creature of libidinous glamour. An example of this is Wilbur Braun's *Aunt Tillie Goes to Town* (1937), in which that eponymous lady starts off 'as a tall, angular woman . . . decidedly stern in manner, sharp in speech' whose 'characteristic is to fold her hands and let them rest in front of her'. By the end of the play, for no very good reason, she doffs her high-necked Victorian garb and takes to beach pyjamas and a Spanish comb. Peggy Fernway's *Life at Aunt Minnie's* (1944) presents a woman of similar physical type to Aunt Tillie who encounters her lost teenage love and takes to wearing long earrings and putting a flower in her hair in order to win him back. In Elsa Kalen's *Aunt Lizzie Lives It Up* (1954), 'a wealthy and eccentric spinster . . . buttoned-up, decidedly stern in manner' takes her niece off on a river cruise and falls off the boat. Because her clothes are ruined, she is lent some naval attire, which she finds liberating. 'Ever since they fished me out of the water, I've been doing a lot of thinking,' she laments. 'All I ever did was work and make money. I've never known what it is to have a good time.' She proposes marriage to the captain and announces brightly, 'I'll dance every night and be belle of the ball.' *

Several aunt plays involve drag. In Andrew Jameson's *His Name Was Aunt Nellie* (1942), the married man Archie slips off to the Saratoga races pretending to his wife that he is visiting his Aunt Nellie, formerly a burlesque queen and no-good woman. Archie's daughter wants to marry the impecunious young actor Jerry, who knows of Archie's deceit, and while the latter is away Jerry dresses up as Aunt Nellie in order to gain access to his girlfriend. More bizarre than this is *Aunt Edwina* by William Douglas-Home, written in 1959 in the wake of the much-advertised case of the first modern transsexual Christine Jorgensen. Here a happily married DSO living respectably in the Home Counties becomes a woman. His tolerant wife airily tells their shocked daughter, 'These things happen every day. They're in the papers practically every morning.' But the girl is embarrassed, to say the least, and in order to avoid humiliation tries to pass her father off to her suitor as Aunt Edwina.

Another common theme, also traceable to *Charley's Aunt*, is that of the aunt who pays a visit from a distant part of the country or abroad. In Madalene Demarest Barnum's *Our Aunt from California* (1903), three impoverished sisters anxiously await

---

* Flora Poste's Aunt Ada Doom undergoes a similar transformation in Stella Gibbons's perfect comic novel *Cold Comfort Farm* (1932). Having confined herself to the solitude of her Sussex farmhouse bedroom for twenty years following the traumatizing glimpse of 'something nasty in the woodshed', Aunt Ada finally admits the briskly practical and urbane Flora to her presence. They have an uninterrupted nine-hour conversation, the substance of which is never revealed. Shortly afterwards, Aunt Ada emerges all smiles, clad in 'the smartest flying kit of black leather', and boards a small aeroplane bound for Paris.

the arrival of their wealthy and eccentric Aunt Merry, who wants a companion for her forthcoming trip to Europe. Andrew Jameson's *Aunt Sally from Cherry Valley* (1947) weaves in the transformation joke. Aunt Sally, 'a crusty old maid . . . tart and plain spoken in her speech but withal rather likable', promises to set up a trust fund for her niece Georgia on the day she marries. She arrives in New York to meet Georgia's new husband, but the husband doesn't actually exist, because Georgia was jilted at the altar. Desperate for money to start up a Fifth Avenue beauty salon, Georgia borrows her business partner's husband Antoine to pretend he is married to her. Antoine charms the old lady and gives her the full treatment, turning her into a vamp with red toenails. Maybe you had to be there – it doesn't sound riotously hilarious.

The most recent play of any note to use an aunt as a central figure was Ray Cooney and John Chapman's 'comedy thriller' *My Giddy Aunt* (1970). Set on a tea estate in India, it shows two scheming nephews plotting against their deluded Aunt Hester, a vehicle for the inimitable Irene Handl and her gift for playing dotty.

Aunts no longer command much interest in the theatre, but they won't quite lie down and die. In 2004, an Off-Broadway theatre presented a new play by Miriam Jensen Hendrix called *When Aunt Daphne Went Nude*, a quaint nostalgic pastiche with a twist. It's 1934, and Reginald Walmesley, rising star of the Foreign Office, wants to marry Emily, a sweet girl from Vermont. Among the factors preventing the match are Emily's Aunt Millicent, who controls her money, and the anti-Semitic Daphne, who thinks Adolf Hitler is a darling and strips off in the name of Nazi naturism and the body beautiful. It ran, not surprisingly, for less than a month and has not been heard of since.

So much for the fiction. Memoirs from the Victorian and Edwardian periods are rich in real aunts who fall somewhere along the axis that leads from Rose Macaulay's Aunt Dot to P. G. Wodehouse's Aunt Agatha. Among the most endearing is Aunt Etty, in Gwen Raverat's delightful memoir of her Cambridge childhood *Period Piece*. Born in 1843, Etty was the eldest daughter of Charles Darwin, and although she was married and survived to a great age, her life was one of unimaginable supine idleness:

> She told me, when she was eighty-six, that she had never made a pot of tea in her life; and that she had never in all her days been out in the dark alone, not even in a cab; and I don't believe she had ever travelled by train without a maid. She certainly always took her maid with her when she went in a fly to the dentist's. She once asked me to give her a bit of the dark meat of a chicken, because she had never tasted anything but the breast. I am sure that she had never sewn on a button, and I should guess that she had hardly ever even posted a letter herself . . . Once she wrote when her maid, the faithful and patient Janet, was away for a day or two 'I am very busy answering my own bell'.

She was one of those Victorian lady valetudinarians, who remain invalid all their lives with an illness or condition that is never specified or diagnosed. When she was thirteen and suffering from 'a low fever', the doctor recommended her to have breakfast in bed for a time. The result was that 'she never got up to breakfast again in all her life'. Her ill health became 'her profession and absorbing interest', Raverat continues.

> But her interest was never tinged by self-pity, it was an abstract, almost scientific interest; and our sympathy was not demanded . . . she was always going away to rest, in case she might be tired later on in the day, or even next day. She would send down to the cook to ask her to count the prune-stones left on her plate, as it was very important to know whether she had eaten three or four prunes at luncheon. She would make Janet put a silk handkerchief over her left foot as she lay in bed, because it was that amount colder than her right foot. And when there were colds about she often wore a kind of gas mask of her own invention. It was an ordinary wire kitchen strainer, stuffed with antiseptic cotton wool, and tied on like a snout, with elastic over her ears. In this she would receive her visitors and discuss politics in a hollow voice out of her eucalyptus-scented seclusion oblivious of the fact that they might be struggling with fits of laughter.

Nevertheless, her nieces and nephews adored her: 'to us she only showed her immense interest in everything in the world, her vitality, her affection'. And despite her frailty, Etty was a woman of passionate convictions and a taste for controversy. Her loathing of Catholicism was particularly fierce. 'If you want a novel to hot you up against the Catholics, I've got a most shocking one here,' she told her niece.

ME: 'Well, I don't really need one just now, thank you; but what's it about?'

AUNT ETTY: 'It's about a priest who rides so fast to give a man absolution before he dies, that he KILLS his horse under him. Isn't it horrible?'

ME (mildly): 'Well, I suppose they believe that absolution matters more than anything else.'

AUNT ETTY (almost unable to speak with indignation): 'But doesn't the Horse matter? Doesn't Cruelty matter? How can they think' etc., etc

Other subjects calculated to get her going included Admiral Jellicoe, Winston Churchill and H. G. Wells. 'Sometimes she would say to one of us "Now you must be Churchill, or Wells, or the Pope of Rome [or anyone else who was out of favour] and just you try to answer a few questions I shall put to you." And then the most devastating questions would be fired off: "How on earth did you expect to take the Dardanelles?" or "You must surely agree that Adultery is wrong?" or "How can you think that confession can strengthen anyone's sense of responsibility?"'

Another breed of aunts in this era was not so much eccentric as exotic: these were the ones who got away, the ones who broke the rules and did not opt for respectability, thus developing an aura of adventure and romance about them. Cecil Beaton describes one such in his autobiographical *My Bolivian Aunt*. In connection with a speculation, the Bolivian entrepreneur Pedro Suarez visited the Westmorland home of Beaton's maternal family in the early 1890s and fell in love with Cecil's Aunt Jessie. Although Suarez was public-school educated and had top-drawer connections, the romance caused a great scandal – similar to that surrounding poor Lilia Herriton in E. M. Forster's *Where Angels Fear to Tread* – and once they were married, they headed back to South America, leaving Jessie's reputation in the Lake District tarnished, if not disgraced.

After several years of letters reporting that she was crossing pontoon bridges on the back of a mule and eating grilled monkey for dinner, Jessie returned to England in style when her husband, having made a fortune in the rubber rush, was appointed head of the Bolivian Legation. To the susceptible young Cecil, she was a figure of extravagant glamour, speaking English with a thick Spanish accent and waving her hands about in a 'continental' manner. She had a pet marmoset and chihuahua, she nibbled on olives and *marrons glacés*, she smoked, she danced the tango and turkey trot, and for trips to the seaside, she donned gym shoes and covered her face with cold cream.

Most startling of all were her clothes. Eschewing the 'soft pale tints of the sweet pea' that the Edwardians considered pretty and decorous, she went for outright brilliance, crowning her outfits with hats that were 'gigantic cartwheels with tall crowns from which sprouted a firework display of osprey, birds of paradise or huge funeral ostrich plumes' (these remained filed in Beaton's mind until they re-emerged fifty years later when he was designing *My Fair Lady*).

But all this wonderful gaiety and energy concealed her unhappiness at her husband's persistent infidelities. The couple returned to Bolivia, but eventually, at the end of her tether, she returned to England without him, claiming that she had been widowed. In a small flat in Maida Vale, she continued to be merry, dining off what was then an unimaginably bizarre cuisine of *arroz a la Valenciana*, *empanadas*, *churros*, *membrillo* and *masaco*, as well as gamely posing in the remnants of her South American finery for her nephew's first photographic portraits. As she became poorer, she grew correspondingly more resourceful and her spirit was undaunted even by the excruciating cancer of the jaw which killed her. She emanated, writes Beaton in tribute, 'a warmer atmosphere of love and friendship than almost any human being I have known'.

RACHEL TOWNSEND ON HER AUNT EMILY CAROLINE KINGTON-BLAIR-OLIPHANT OF ARDBLAIR

My maiden aunt on my mother's side was Emily. Most families can boast of one eccentric. Em was ours.

Handsome in a classic style, she was vain of her looks and especially of her white skin. I never saw her hatless out-of-doors, or without a large parasol on sunny days. Neither did I see her normally dressed, but always wearing some fantastic and eye-catching frippery, as unsuitable to the mediaeval castle which was her Scottish home, as to the little house in London where she spent her last years.

In the nineties, it was fashionable for sisters to dress alike, so Em's peculiar taste in clothes did not become apparent until her sisters married. As the one daughter left at home, her wildest fancies could be indulged, for my grandmother, finding remonstrance useless, took the line of least resistance. The scraps of velvet, the ragged lace, the huge paste necklaces and ear-rings, the high-heeled pale satin shoes, and the picture hats which Em loved and always wore, were a mingled source of amusement and humiliation to her family. She would join the guns at a shooting luncheon wearing a woolen skirt, a pink satin blouse, a lace bolero, several pieces of imitation jewellery, and a pair of diamond-buckled shoes, to the astonishment of the local sportsmen and the other women guests in their conventional sober tweeds and stout brogues; and many a time I have seen passers-by doing their unsuccessful best to hide their smiles as Em scurried rapidly by. (Her walk was almost a run.) It was embarrassing for children to be seen in public with this extraordinary figure, and yet we all enjoyed her company. She noticed the staring strangers, but thought she was merely arousing admiration, for in her own view, no-one knew how to dress but herself. One of her loyal nephews, aged fifteen, once fought a boy whom he had seen laughing at her in a tea-shop. Em, although surprised by his unexplained violence, remained serenely unaware of its cause.

She never used cosmetics or dyed her untidy white hair, but as she grew older the bits and pieces which covered her gaunt form became even more bizarre, and she designed a series of terrible outfits, beloved by her but dreaded by all her relations. We had nicknames for some of them, and before any family wedding we used to hold sweepstakes on what Em would wear for the occasion. There was Toreador, a dashing red cloak with Spanish hat; baby mine, high-waisted white muslin with blue ribbons; Sea Caves, pastel chiffon hung with iridescent sea shells and sea weed; and several nameless atrocities in vivid brocade with panels of contrasting sateen.

Em's ideas for dresses were carried out by a village dressmaker in Scotland, but heaven knows what dauntless milliner

made her hats. I do know, however, that they would not fit into any normal hat-box, and that she had enormous cardboard boxes especially made for them.

Em's arrival at the railway station on a country-house visit was (my mother used to say) a humbling sight. Besides the large trunks and cardboard boxes, there was a little matter of seven old umbrellas which always accompanied her, and she usually wore a tattered black brocade cloak, long since discarded by my grandmother as being too old for her. Beneath a vast Gainsborough hat, her happy smiling face looked out, and all one's sense of outraged convention was lost in a rush of affection. Even the porters struggling with her difficult luggage were her willing slaves before the end of the platform was reached.

For everybody loved Em. No picture of her would be complete which did not make that clear. I never saw her cross or even ruffled. But always sunny and warm-hearted, generous to the point of silliness, and well-bred in the essence of her being. Even in her amazing appearance, that shone out. Mad, a stranger would have said, but a mad aristocrat.

Em's chief interest, after clothes, was in writing. Year after year, she bombarded editors with jejune essays, sentimental stories and poems which never quite scanned. None was ever accepted, but she scribbled happily on in her large angular handwriting, signing her works with all five of her names in full. In addition, she would enter at least one literary competition every week. Occasionally an extract from her entry would be mockingly quoted, and then she was enchanted at having been noticed. She was never cast down, and continued to the end of her life to think of herself as a writer.

She also considered herself to be a connoisseur of female

beauty. It was a harmless enough notion, except that she loyally fancied her nieces to be lovely beyond compare. This nonsense embarrassed and exasperated us all, especially as she took the view that no men were good enough for us, and our perfectly suitable engagements were greeted by a disappointed sigh. My mother told me that Em had been even worse in her youth, holding that nobody was a grand enough match for her brilliant sisters, and saying so to anyone who would listen. Her two brothers-in-law had consequently a good deal to forgive. She forgot her disapproval, however, when babies came along. Em loved children (though her affection took the form, so dreaded by nannies, of over-feeding and over-exciting them) and she gradually became reconciled to the fact that their fathers were neither royal nor even ducal.

After my grandmother's death, Em left Scotland and went to live in London. At first she found a haven in an obscure boarding house (my Zoo, she called it) where she made friends with a number of elderly oddities. 'It's a shame,' I remember her saying, 'there's a dear old lady in my Zoo whose selfish daughter never takes her out anywhere. I shall take her to luncheon in a nice restaurant.' And she did but only once, because in the middle of the meal, the excited old lady suddenly gave an eldritch shriek and tore off all her clothes. 'Still, she enjoyed her treat,' said Em blandly afterwards.

Later Em took a charming little mews cottage in Belgravia. She would never allow anyone into her bedroom, which was piled to the ceiling with old newspapers, hat-boxes, manuscripts and dust, but the rest of the house was perfunctorily cleaned by a series of disreputable women who were experts at getting money out of her. Here she lived in the way she really enjoyed, turning night into day. She stayed in bed through most of the daylight hours, and getting up in the evenings, she would trot off to a restaurant and then to a late cinema, returning to read or write till dawn. It was disconcerting to have a daytime engagement with Em, for she almost always fell asleep, and one hostess, I remember, after Em had dozed and nodded throughout a tea-party, bade her farewell with a grim smile and the words 'Goodbye, Emily, I do hope you'll have a good night.'

Most film actors were grist to Em's romantic mill, but one star outshone the rest. It was Rudolph Valentino. We all felt that the adoration of this ageing woman for the young actor was too pathetic to be amusing, but when after his death Em somehow acquired his Cossack hat and wore it all over London, our mortification overcame our sense of pity. We would have preferred the Gainsborough creations, but there was no holding Em; she worshipped him, and we had to put up with it. After all, we had been used all our lives to seeing Em in fancy dress.

One of her favourite occupations in London was attending the weddings of perfect strangers and afterwards denigrating the dresses, but her happiest outings were to watch royal processions. She would somehow manage to keep awake for these, and would always contrive to have an excellent view. One of her nephews, a young officer in the Guards, said that he never took part in any ceremony without wondering if he would see Em on top of a lamp-post. What with weddings, processions and cinemas, her life in London was full of interest, and I am certain that it completely satisfied her.

Em had a comfortable fortune, but no money sense at all, and as the years went on, her capital dwindled in a way that would have alarmed anyone less blithe than she. Her sisters *found that giving her money was useless (my mother discovered that Em was supporting, among other beggars, the lover of her last charwoman but two) and that the only way to ensure her comfort was to pay the landlord and the grocer direct. For years her little house had become a magnet for spongers and idlers and when she died she was very nearly penniless. She was ill for months, but she never complained and with incredible pluck and spirit she went gamely to her end.*

I never knew what became of the Cossack hat.

Auntie

(D. Eardley Wilmot, 1923)

I once was fascinated by a charming
    millionaire
I knew he thought me rather nice, with
    heaps of savoir-faire
But auntie grew seductive as she
    played the chaperone
And she carried off the bull's eye
Leaving me behind to moan
Auntie is a darling, Auntie is so smart
Auntie knows the sort of ways
That win the rich man's heart.

6

X-Rated Aunts

In my student days, I remember a Casanovan friend confiding that he prevented his physical ardour from reaching an over-hasty conclusion by forcing himself, at the crucial moment, to envisage a row of over-filled dustbins. A line-up of his elderly aunts might well have performed a similar function, for sex and aunts don't go together. Indeed they seem to cancel each other out, as they do in the absurdly oxymoronic title of Mavis Cheek's novel *The Sex Life of My Aunt* (2002), though what the story actually shows is how wrong one can be in one's assumptions about the respectability of elderly relations.

Yet of all the stereotypes that characterize the breed, there is perhaps none so vivid as the pathetically shrivelled maiden aunt who conceives a hopeless crush on a man younger and more attractive than she is. A painful example of this is provided by *Curious Relations* (1945), a blackly hilarious but sadly forgotten fictional autobi-ography by William Plomer, writ-ing under the pseudonym of William D'Arfey. The book focus-es on two intermarried families, the D'Arfeys and the Mountfaucons, of equal if differing degrees of lunacy.

One of the more notable characters among the Mountfaucons (prone, in alternate generations, to dipsomania and epilepsy) is unmarried, unloved Aunt Chrissie. Diminutive and stout, grouchy and short of external charms, she has twice been disappointed by the objects of her infatuation, the second of them being a keen cyclist, who has bequeathed her an aching fixation on that means of transport. She also seeks solace in eating.

Unfortunately the extremely plain cooking at Holderfield did not afford her the variety for which she craved. One evening when there was no one about she borrowed the housemaid's cycle without a word and proceeded to pedal off hot-foot to the nearest shops in the suburb of Langholme, some miles distant, where she made a remarkable variety of purchases. Slices of ham, tinned pineapple chunks, Swiss rolls, doughnuts, bath buns, mixed biscuits, sausage rolls, candied peel, foie gras, chocolate éclairs, bottles of ginger beer and several currant loaves were all packed into her carriers. Adding to these some tinned lobster and salmon, she rode peacefully home, hid the bicycle, and sneaked up the back stairs to her room. The dressing gong sounded, and it was assumed she was already in her room; the dinner gong pealed, but there was no sign of her. Constantia dispatched a footman to look for her; he knocked on Chrissie's door, but there was no answer; he tried it, only to find it locked. He came downstairs and told my step-grandmother, who ordered the butler to force the door. This was duly done, and revealed my tiny aunt prone on the floor in a coma, a tin-opener grasped firmly in her hand. Around her lay a mixed debris of empty tins and paper bags, fragments of sausage and pastry, crumbs of cake and empty éclair cases, from which the coffee icing and the cream had been licked, and pieces of orange peel. The mess was indescribable, but for the first time in its existence Aunt Chrissie's ugly room had taken on an air of debauched joviality; it looked like Hampstead Heath after a Bank Holiday . . .

Christine lay in the centre of the shattered still-life in much the same condition as a little born bear at the Zoo after an orgy of buns; the buttons of her tightly fitting corsage strained their threads by her steady expansion; she was blown out like a balloon.  Her expression, as she lay there, was rapturous, a general warning not to despise the happiness of others.

When she recovers, she denies eating anything at all. "'What!" she exclaimed. "Me do a thing like that? A well brought-up bicycle like *me*?'"

Later she became quite normal again, but was, of course, more closely watched than ever; but after a long space of time, she again found the means to slip out and go shopping once more. This time her purchases were on a more Trimalchian scale than before.

When at length they found her it was for the last time.
She was lying on her bed in an incredible litter, her face
smeared with jam and Devonshire cream, with the straw-
boater which she had worn for nearly a quarter of a century
on the back of her head, with an already faded bunch of
pink and blue hydrangeas pinned to it. A fire was still
smouldering in the grate, while the tiled hearth was piled
up with a mass of broken glass and charred rubbish of all
sorts. On a closer inspection, the fire proved to have been
composed of the photographs of all her relatives, and of the
innumerable pietistic tracts and works with which her
book-cases were liberally stacked. Every single one had
been destroyed. Her fragile body, swollen in its hideous
black dress, was spotted with crumbs and sherbet powder;
but on her face was an expression of unutterable peace and
repose; all its lines, all the footprints of time had been
smoothed away. In death she had recaptured some of her
childish prettiness – and something more . . .

This is typical of the grotesque humiliation that the maiden
aunt faces when she dares to give way to romantic yearnings.
But there is another role which an aunt can play, one which
presents her in a more alluring light: as the initiator into the
world of adult pleasures. In Colette's short story *Gigi* (1944),
the teenage heroine is groomed by her Aunt Alicia, an elderly
courtesan whose attitudes are entirely worldly. Alicia is scheming for Gigi to be set up as the mistress of Gaston, the playboy
son of her former amour, and in anticipation of her forthcoming pampered existence spends hours teaching the girl the
finer points of table manners, such as the proper way to eat

lobster. But ironically all Aunt Alicia's best-laid plans go wrong when Gaston and Gigi reject the morality of their forefathers by falling in love and deciding to get married.

For aunts and nephews, initiation can take a more physical turn, with the nephew's adolescent libido taking the lead. Their sexual intercourse is not always against the law. Incest between aunt and nephew is not a strongly defined taboo, though the source of all Judaeo-Christian legislation, Leviticus 18, where the Lord spake unto Moses, decrees:

12 Thou shalt not uncover the nakedness of thy father's sister; she is thy father's near kinswoman.

13 Thou shalt not uncover the nakedness of the mother's sister; for she is thy near kinswoman.

Almost universally, a niece or nephew is forbidden from marrying an uncle or aunt to whom they have any blood relation or 'consanguinity' – the principal exception being the strongly matrilineal Trobriand Islands, where sexual relations with your father's sister are not considered incestuous. (In France and Italy, presidential or parliamentary decree can in exceptional circumstances permit the marriage of aunt and nephew or uncle and niece, but I have been unable to discover what these circumstances might be or whether any such decree has ever been issued.) Equally widespread is the freedom to marry a widowed or divorced aunt or uncle to whom there is no blood link. Hence Mario Vargas Llosa's novel *Aunt Julia and the Scriptwriter* (1977) isn't as scandalous as it sounds. It's really only the Stendhalian-Colettique tale of a guileless young man in love with a sophisticated older woman:

the hero, a minor, ends up marrying his uncle's wife's sister, an aunt only by extension of the normal usage.[*]

Pornographic literature doesn't get as excited about incest along the aunt–nephew axis as it does about mother–son or brother–sister relations, but it's a lively enough fantasy none the less, as the thousands of true-life confessions on many repellent modern websites can evince. Somewhat more engaging in tone is *Forbidden Fruit*, a novel dating from 1898, in which pretty young Aunt Gertie arrives to look after her twelve-year-old nephew Percy, a lad with one thing on his mind. Owing to the smallness of the house, he is obliged to share his bedroom with her. After the light has been turned out, she creeps in. 'What a beautiful boy,' she coos over his bed, thinking him to be asleep. 'If only I dared . . .'

> She leans down and kisses him. Percy wakes up and kisses his aunt back.
>
> 'What a silly spooney boy you are, Percy, I thought you were asleep.'
>
> 'Oh no, Aunt Gertie, I do love you so, and when you kissed me I could not help paying you back. Don't you love me a little?'
>
> 'Now go to sleep, there's a good boy. I must go to bed myself, put your head under the clothes. If I catch you peeping at me, I'll whip your bottom, that's all.'
>
> Her trickle in the chamber pot arouses him. 'How funny

---

[*] Shakespeare's Hamlet, already suffering from a bad case of the Oedipus complex, is further confused when his widowed mother Gertrude marries his late father's brother Claudius, making them 'my uncle-father and aunt-mother', as he puts it to Rosencrantz and Guildenstern (*Hamlet*, II.ii).

the noise of your pee-pee has made me feel, I am all of a tremble,' he says.

So one things leads to another, and eventually aunt and nephew are locked in intimate congress. 'Percy, push yourself closer to me, it's so nice, my darling,' whispers Aunt Gertie. 'A kind of rage possessed me,' Percy recalls. 'I wanted to kill her by thrusting my instrument as savagely as possible.'

Following a climax and detumescence, Percy moans, 'Oh, Auntie, you've killed me, it's gone dead now.' 'Don't call me Auntie,' she replies. 'Call me Gertie. Say you love me, Percy, but never tell anyone what we have done tonight.'

After further copulation and some playful spanking, Gertie cries: 'Percy, what a champion you are,' and christens him 'Mr Pego'. But the triumphant Percy now has another conquest in mind – his even more lubricious mother. Enough said.

In 1909–11, desperately attempting to make some money at the beginning of his literary career, Guillaume Apollinaire wrote several essays in pornography, now considered by connoisseurs to be little gems of erotica. 'So limpidly perverse, so fragrant with young private perfumes that one wonders if it may not be another of [his] anti-Symbolist sallies,' wrote his biographer Francis Steegmuller of *Les Exploits d'un jeune Don Juan*. Roger, a wealthy pubescent, is sent to live in a deserted chateau with his mother, sisters and aunt.

In childhood, he had been bathed of an evening by his twenty-six-year-old Aunt Marguerite, who was ten years younger than his mother. 'I remember vividly that every time my Aunt Marguerite washed and dried my genitals I was conscious of an unfamiliar vague but extremely pleasant sensation,' he writes.

'Come now, auntie, wash my prickly pear as well.'

'Shame on you, you bad little boy. You are perfectly capable of washing it yourself.'

'No, auntie, please, you wash it. I can't do it nearly as well as you can.' And taking the sponge, she carefully washed my cock and balls.

'Oh the little rascal, let me give you a great big kiss for being so kind,' I said.

And I kissed her pretty cherry-red lips behind which sparkled her beautiful white teeth.

As soon as I was out of the bath, I begged her to dry me. So my aunt dried me, lingering perhaps even longer than was necessary over my sensitive areas.

At that point, prim Aunt Marguerite decides that the fun has gone far enough. But Roger wants more – 'Be a nice auntie and have a bath with me some time.' Auntie resists, at which Roger resorts to blackmail: 'If you don't, I'll tell Daddy that you've put my thing in your mouth again.'

My aunt blushed deeply. As a matter of fact, she really had done that, but only for a second, one day when I had not wanted to take my bath. The water had been too cold and I'd run off to my room to hide. May aunt had come looking for me and at length had taken my tiny penis into her mouth, squeezing it between her lips for a second. I had enjoyed it so much that I had finally relented and become as docile as a lamb.

Eventually, to keep the boy quiet, Aunt Marguerite agrees to get into the bath alone. Roger helps her to dry and dress.

I got down on my knees and wiped my aunt's dainty feet. When I wiped between her toes she laughed and when I touched and tickled the soles of her feet her humour returned and she agreed to let me dry her calves.

As he reaches her knees, however, she stops him, and henceforth he and his aunt take their baths separately. But a few days later, Roger overhears her in the confessional, admitting in low and hesitant tones

that although she had never before felt any carnal desires, she had been moved to emotion upon seeing her young nephew in his bath, and had lustfully touched his body, but fortunately had been able to master these wicked desires. Except once when her nephew was sleeping; the blanket had slipped off the bed, leaving his genitals exposed. She had stood there looking at him for a long time and had even taken his member into her mouth.

The priest naturally takes lubricious interest in this tale:

The Confessor: Haven't you ever sinned with men, or haven't you ever polluted yourself when alone?

My Aunt: I remain a virgin, at least as far as men are concerned. I've often looked at myself in the mirror, and fondled my private parts with my hand. Once . . . (she hesitated)

> *The Confessor*: Courage, my child, conceal nothing from your confessor.

Et cetera. Some weeks later, after he has had his way with several other ladies of low estate, Roger discovers his aunt in the chateau's library, reading the entry in the encyclopedia for 'onanism' and looking at the *Atlas of Anatomy*.

> I pretended not to notice her embarrassment, and said to her softly: 'You too must get bored sometimes, auntie dear. The priest who lived here before had quite a collection of interesting books dealing with the problems of human life. Why don't you take some with you to your room?'
>
> I took two and slipped them into her pocket: *Marriage Unveiled* and *Love and Marriage*. When she affected reluctance, I added: 'Naturally, this is between you and me and the gatepost: we're not children are we, auntie?' And I suddenly seized her and gave her a resounding kiss.

The boy is soon transported with ardour, and Marguerite is forced to resist his advances again. But when they next meet alone, the citadel falls. Roger slips into her bedroom and he blurts out his passion for her. 'Let us be husband and wife, beautiful, darling Marguerite.' She succumbs, and what follows is 'a brief encounter, but one whose sensations were infinite' which 'brought both of us to the limit of the most frenzied ecstasy'. After this first bout, they are immediately at it again, in 'a long battle during which we perspired through every pore in our bodies. Shouting like a mad woman, she was the first to reach the climax. Mine felt so good that it almost hurt. That was enough; we separated.'

At the novel's conclusion, it is revealed that both the aunt and another of Roger's conquests are pregnant. Husbands are found to make their position respectable, and Roger continues to enjoy extra-marital sessions with both of them. Apollinaire, in case you are wondering, didn't have an aunt.

Such is the stuff of idle masturbatory fantasy. To find a truly perceptive account of the relationship between an aunt and a nephew, we must turn to Stendhal's rambling but enthralling novel *La Chartreuse de Parme* ('The Charterhouse of Parma'), published in 1839. It's the story of a young nobleman called Fabrice del Dongo, who returns to his home in northern Italy after fighting for Napoleon at Waterloo. He comes back, covered with some sort of glory, and his mother's sister Gina – the Countess Pietranera, and then on her remarriage the Duchess of Sanseverina, a woman of beauty, vivacity, intelligence and will – is enchanted by him. No, more than enchanted – disarmed and confused. Not having any children of her own, she had adored Fabrice as a boy, but now she adores him as a handsome young man, and something unfamilial infects her attachment, something which she cannot openly acknowledge. 'If he had spoken of love, she would have loved him,' the narrator explains. To Fabrice, however, she is still nothing more than his beloved aunt, and his 'embraces overflowed with such innocent gratitude and artless affection that she would have been horrified at herself had she looked for another sentiment in that almost filial attachment'. (Owing to doubts that hang over Fabrice's parentage, it is never totally clear that Gina is Fabrice's aunt, though the novel never positively reveals otherwise.)

Gina becomes the mistress of the politician Count Mosca, a man of wise and mature perceptions who loves her deeply. But

she cannot leave Fabrice alone: to call him her toyboy would be crude, but not inaccurate. After he murders someone in a brawl, he is in danger of losing his life, but Gina saves him from a death sentence by pleading with the Prince of Parma. She thinks she has secured his release too, but she is double-crossed, and Fabrice is locked up in a prison, where he falls in love with the commandant's daughter, a pretty but insipid young thing called Clelia. Unaware of this, Gina plots Fabrice's escape, putting herself on the line and breaking with Mosca in the process. It is the self-sacrifice of a woman passionately in love and playing every card in her hand at once.

When Fabrice is freed, she rides with him in a coach which will take him to safety. Kind and grateful and attentive though he is, he falls into silent reverie, and Gina realizes that she has lost him. 'It would have happened sooner or later,' she reflects. 'Sorrow has aged me, or perhaps he truly loves someone else, and I now have only second place in his heart.'

Fabrice does not value his freedom; he longs to be back in the prison, which would allow him to be close to Clelia, and surrenders himself. Gina knows that his enemies would like to poison him while he is in prison, and although she has admitted defeat, she makes one final sacrifice on his behalf – her honour. To secure his release and pardon, she prostitutes herself to the Prince of Parma. Destroyed by the humiliation, she leaves Parma and marries Mosca. Clelia is then forced to marry someone else, and in an empty revenge, Gina cannot resist gloating over Fabrice's misery. But she is a broken woman, having lost a battle she could never have won.

A more striking transgression of the taboo is provided by Charlotte Mendelson's *Love in Idleness* (2001), a rather vapid novel written from a lesbian perspective in a manner that lies uneasily between Margaret Drabble and Bridget Jones. Anna is a goofy graduate who doesn't really know much about herself. She finds her middle-class family very irritating and can't wait to get away from home. Only her mother's feline sister Stella holds any sort of fascination for her –the fascination of glamour. Stella's lips look 'as soft as marzipan' and her 'long, cool, crescent-lidded eyes . . . pin you smiling in their gaze'. In personality, she is 'famous for her sneer . . . ironic, unimpressed, and somewhat dangerous. She is never nice for effect, unlike her sister, who doesn't have the courage to be seriously rude.' Mostly she lives in Paris, where she is involved in film-making, and she offers Anna the use of her Bloomsbury house while she is away.

Anna accepts with delight and arrives in London, where she finds a job in a bookshop. But she finds the house-sitting unnerving, not least because of the baffling clues she picks up about her aunt's love life, including a photograph of her amorously entwined with another woman. Eventually Anna meets up with someone she assumes to be Stella's boyfriend, but he makes it clear that this is not the case: Stella is a mystery wrapped inside an enigma.

Stella finally returns to the London house, and she and Anna spend the evening together, talking and drinking as the atmosphere gets headier. What follows might just be the world's first-ever aunt–niece clinch – ground-breaking, if not earth-shattering.

Stella's hand is on her shoulder. She turns to see her picking a piece of cellophane from her heel. 'I think we both know.'

Anna uncertainly meets her eye.

'God, I'm drunk,' says Stella, righting herself.

'Me too.' The hand remains on her shoulder, waiting.

'Stella . . .'

'Yes?'

'Do you know?'

'I think I do.' Her hand gives a little squeeze. She meets her gaze. And then for one long oblivious second, Anna moves into the hot and spinning space between them.

There is a hand on her waist, and her own palm rests on a fluttering curve of skin. She stands on an island, in a storm of fireballs, shooting stars and lightning – a soft electric collision of lips and figures.

Then, gently, Stella disengages. The new world wavers and is lost. 'Anna.'

She clears her throat, and looks up, dazzled. But Stella's face is dark. 'Yes?'

'Oh, Anna.' Anna wedges her nail in a crack in the painted windowframe, and waits, liquefying. Then Stella gives a smile: amusement, and a little sympathy.

Anna digs her nails deep into the ball of her thumb, and forces her head up. 'I –'

'Shhh,' says Stella, touching the side of Anna's cheek with the back of her hand. 'It's OK. Forget it.'

'How? I mean . . .'

'No, really. Just do. It's not an ordinary goodnight kiss, I grant you – but it happens. Both drunk. Don't look so horrified.'

Anna is appalled at herself.

Her mother's sister.

Her mother's *sister*.
Not just her relative.
But female.
Both female.
Oh God, what has she done?

There's a happy ending. Stella vanishes – she's a free spirit, with other, unspecified fish to fry – but arranges for the entwined woman from the photograph (obviously her former girlfriend) to come round and sort Anna out. Whatever next?

Gigolo Aunts

An indie rock band formed in 1986 in Boston, Mass., comprising of Dave Gibbs (vocals/rhythm); Phil Hurley (lead guitar) and his brother Steve Hurley (bass guitar), later replaced by Jon Skibic; and Paul Brouwer (drums), later replaced by Fred Eltringham. Previously calling themselves Sniper, Marauder and Rosetta Stone, they took the name of Gigolo Aunts from an incomprehensible psychedelic song by the mysterious Syd Barrett, one of the founding fathers of Pink Floyd,

> Gigolo Aunt
> Will you please keep on the track
> 'cause I almost want you back
> 'cause I know what you are
> you are a gigolo aunt, you're a gigolo aunt!
> Yes I know what you are
> you are a gigolo aunt, you're a gigolo aunt!

The band remained little known until in 1992, when it was signed up by a small British label, Fire Records. Live, it was most appreciated for cover versions, but *Where I Find My Heaven*, an album of original songs released in 1995, provoked its biggest success – the title track was used both in the first gross-out movie *Dumb and Dumber* and as the theme tune to a BBC sitcom called *Game On*.

Fighting through several contractual problems and changes in personnel, the band has suffered many ups and downs since the peak of its fame, but its artistic emphasis has constantly remained on emotional and musical clarity, pitched very loud. The Gigolo Aunts' style is untricksy and extrovert. 'Cleverness is an overrated commodity' says Dave Gibbs. 'I appreciate irony, but not at the expense of honesty, so we keep our approach pretty direct.'

The Gigolo Aunts' most recent album was *Minor Chords and Major Themes*, released in 2003. Since then the band appears to have disbanded, and Gibbs has gone solo.

7

Damned Bad Aunts

'To be sure, aunts of all kinds are damned bad things,' complains Tony Lumpkin in Oliver Goldsmith's comedy *She Stoops to Conquer* (1773). P. G. Wodehouse's Bertie Wooster (see p. 123–6) would have fervently agreed. Both fellows are, of course, great boobies, prize chumps and laughing stocks. This book prefers to present aunts in a positive light, as beacons of a civilizing, loving kindness, at one remove from the intensely emotional power struggle that underlies parenthood.

But we must not sentimentalize: Tony's and Bertie's viewpoint must be given its due. There are aunts – of all kinds, at all times, in all places – who are indeed damned bad things. Look to the Victorian novel, that great treasury of human nature, for examples. The villain of Charlotte Brontë's *Jane Eyre* is Mrs Reed, the heroine's aunt by marriage. Jane is an orphan, taken into the Reed family by her kindly uncle. After his death, Jane is left as the cuckoo in the nest and demoted to Cinderella status. Being of a stubborn, passionate nature, she cannot bear to call her persecutor 'Aunt' – she remains Mrs Reed, a barrier to life and love. 'I am not your dear,' Jane snaps, when a brief phoney show of auntly affection is made. 'Send me to school soon, Mrs Reed, for I hate to live here.'

Later in the novel, Mrs Reed turns out to have been actively malign. When Jane's rich uncle in Madeira writes offering to adopt her, Mrs Reed tells him that Jane died in the typhus epidemic that swept through Lowood Institution, the hideous Evangelical boarding school where Jane was confined. This is not just spite – Mrs Reed hopes that her children will in consequence inherit John Eyre's fortune. Her nemesis comes when her son turns out to be a bad egg and she is left to endure a painful deathbed. Finding her laid so low, Jane's impulse is to forgive, but Mrs Reed will have none of it and she dies unreconciled.

Elizabeth Barrett Browning's excessively melodramatic and episodic verse novel *Aurora Leigh* was published in 1856, nine years after Jane Eyre, and shows lineaments of its influence. On the death of her hot-blooded Italian mother, the spirited black-eyed Aurora is sent to live with her all too English aunt:

> A nose drawn sharply, yet in delicate lines;
> A close mild mouth, a little soured about
> The ends, through speaking unrequited loves
> Or peradventure niggardly half-truths . . .

She embodies the aunt as desiccated spinster, siphoning what could have been her natural affections into what Barrett Browning calls 'a sort of cage-bird life . . .'

> A harmless life, she called a virtuous life
> A quiet life, which was not life at all

She attempts to drill her niece into following suit, but like Jane Eyre, Aurora gets away, eventually marrying a man blind since his house burnt down.

Not all auntly clutches are escaped. Linda Tressel, the eponymous heroine of Anthony Trollope's little-read novella published anonymously in 1867, has no such luck. Like Jane, she is an orphan. Her Aunt Charlotte, with whom she lives in Nuremberg, is a fanatical Baptist, determined that her niece will marry her lodger, a dreary and conventional middle-aged clerk. Other Trollope novels – *He Knew He Was Right*, for example – show auntly meddling in marital matters eventually being quashed, but in this bleak tale, Linda escapes with a younger man of her choice, only to discover that he is a political insurrectionary wanted by the police. Shamed and cowed, Linda is forced to return to her aunt, and we are left to imagine the rest of their life together.

More subtle is the baneful auntly influence in Henry James's *The Wings of the Dove* (1902), where money rather than morality is the motor. Kate Croy's mother has died and she is left only with her pathetically disgraced but faintly sinister father, who lives in reduced circumstances. Kate's rich Aunt Maud makes it clear that she will leave the girl her fortune, on the condition that she breaks with her father and the man she loves, a mere journalist, to marry somebody socially grand.

Like Oscar Wilde's Lady Bracknell, Aunt Maud has a formidable imperiousness that brooks no opposition; she is entirely materialistic, but no fool.

> She would have made a wonderful lioness for a show, an extraordinary figure in a cage or anywhere; majestic, magnificent, high-coloured, all brilliant gloss, perpetual satin, twinkling bugles and flashing gems, with a lustre of agate eyes, a sheen of raven hair, a polish of complexion that was like that of well-kept china and that – as if the skin were too tight – told especially at curves and corners. Her niece had a quiet name for her – she kept it quiet, thinking of her,

with a free fancy, as somehow typically insular, she talked to herself of Britannia of the Market Place – Britannia unmistakeable but with a pen in her ear – and felt she should not be happy till she might on some occasion add to the rest of the panoply a helmet, a shield, a trident and a ledger.

The force of one aunt is as nothing, however, against the power of two or more – the gaggle of aunts, pincer-clawed or tentacular. Today such an image immediately evokes two cartoon figures, Bart Simpson's dreadful pair of aunts, sisters to his mother, the amiable downtrodden Marge. The cynical chain-smoking Selma Bouvier loathes her brother-in-law Homer implacably, but there may be an element of jealousy in this: her own two marriages ended in failure. Sideshow Bob had served time in jail for his attempt to frame Krusty the Clown before he tried to blow Selma up on their honeymoon. She then moved on to a two-bit movie actor, Troy McClure, whom she married after his involvement in a scandal involving underage fish. Their union did not last long, and Selma now devotes herself to Jub Jub, her pet iguana. Patty Bouvier, another chain-smoker, is simply a vacuum whose job is administering eye tests for the Springfield Department of Motor Vehicles. To Bart and his sister Lisa, aunts represent nothing but trouble.

They would have sympathized with Hector and Ethel Munro. Some 120 years before *The Simpsons*, these real-life siblings were sent to live with their Aunt Charlotte, known as Tom, and Aunt Augusta in North Devon, while their father served in the military police in Burma. Their house was fetid, as they mistrusted fresh air, and the atmosphere was further

poisoned by the two women's mutual loathing and ceaseless bickering. Ethel later recalled that 'Aunt Tom had no scruples' and 'never saw when she was hurting people's feelings . . . she was a colossal humbug and never knew it'; the hypochondriacal Aunt Augusta had 'a talent for being able to work herself into a passion over the most trivial annoyance'.

What made young Hector's and Ethel's lives doubly miserable was their aunts' feud, which extended to the boundaries of domestic discipline. 'We could not obey both aunts,' Ethel remembered. 'I believe each gave us orders which she knew were contrary to those issued by the other.' One forbade walking on grass, the other told them to keep off the gravel.

Both aunts were keen on religion, but neither of them 'permitted it to come between her and her ruling passion, which was to outwit the other'. What they squabbled about never seemed to be of much importance. If Aunt Tom came back from Barnstaple market bearing reports of poultry she had bought for 2s. 6d., Aunt Augusta would know no peace until she had seen a far fitter bird at 2s. 4d. Then a row began – more or less intense, according to the length of time that had elapsed since the last one.

'We often longed for revenge,' recalled Ethel, 'with an intensity I suspect we inherited from our Highland ancestry,' and when they had escaped and grown up, Hector took it, deliciously so. Under the *nom de plume* of Saki, he became the author of very short, very bitchy stories with a sting in their tail, filling them with ludicrously stupid and unpleasant aunts, many of whom meet terrible ends or reversals of fortune. In 'The Lumber Room', for example, a damned bad aunt calls out to her nephew Nicholas to rescue her. 'I've been looking for you in the gooseberry garden, and I've slipped into the rain-water tank,' she explains.

'Luckily there's no water in it, but the sides are slippery and I can't get out. Fetch the little ladder from under the cherry tree –'

'I was told I wasn't to go into the gooseberry garden,' said Nicholas promptly.

'I told you not to, and now I tell you that you may,' came the voice from the rain-water tank, rather impatiently.

'Your voice doesn't sound like aunt's,' objected Nicholas; 'You may be the Evil One tempting me to be disobedient. Aunt often tells me that the Evil One tempts me and that I always yield. This time I'm not going to yield.'

'Don't talk nonsense,' said the prisoner in the tank; 'go and fetch the ladder.'

'Will there be strawberry jam for tea?' asked Nicholas innocently.

'Certainly there will be,' said the aunt, privately resolving that Nicholas should have none of it.

'Now I know that you are the Evil One and not aunt,' shouted Nicholas gleefully; 'when we asked aunt for strawberry jam yesterday she said there wasn't any. I know there are four jars of it in the store cupboard, because I looked, and of course you know it's there, but she doesn't, because she said there wasn't any. Oh Devil, you *have* sold yourself.'

There was an unusual sense of luxury in being able to talk to an aunt as though one was talking to the Evil One, but Nicholas knew, with childish discernment, that such luxuries were not to be over-indulged in. He walked noisily away, and it was a kitchen-maid, in search of parsley, who eventually rescued the aunt from the rain-water tank.

Hector and Ethel Munro at least had each other for consolation. Augustus Hare was more at the mercy of his aunts. A prolific writer of travel books who also penned a six-volume autobiography, *The Story of My Life* (published in 1896–1900 and thought to be of record-breaking length), Hare was an only child with an adoptive mother dependent on her sisters' charity. Aunt Lucy 'was a very refined person and a very charming and delightful companion to those she loved, and had she loved me, I should have been devoted to her,' he admits. However, 'having heard some one say that I was more intelligent than [her son] little Marcus, [she] had conceived the most violent jealousy of me, and I was cowed and snubbed by her in every possible way.' Much, much worse was his Aunt Esther, otherwise the formidable Mrs Julius Hare, wife of the Archdeacon of Lewes and sister to the founder of Christian socialism F. D. Maurice, to whom Augustus's mother was beholden. Every night, Augustus and his mother were called upon to dine at the Archdeacon's rectory. It was 'absolute purgatory' for the boy, and it traumatized him.

> I was generally left in a dark room till dinner at seven o'clock, for candles were never allowed in winter in the room where I was left alone. After dinner I was never permitted to amuse myself, or to do anything . . . If I spoke, Aunt Esther would say with a satirical smile, 'As if you could ever say anything worth hearing, as if it was ever possible that one could want to hear what you have to say.' If I took up a book, I was told instantly to put it down again, it

was 'disrespect to my Uncle.' If I murmured, Aunt Esther, whose temper was absolutely unexcitable, quelled it by her icy rigidity. Thus gradually I got into the habit of absolute silence at the Rectory – a habit which it took me years to break through; and I often still suffer from the want of self-confidence engendered by reproaches and taunts which never ceased: for a day – for a week – for a year they would have been nothing: but for *always*, with no escape but my own death or that of my tormentor! Water dripping for ever on a stone wears through the stone at last.

The cruelty was not only mental but physical.

I was a very delicate child, and suffered absolute agonies from chilblains, which were often two large open wounds on my feet. Therefore, I was put to sleep in 'the barracks' – two dismal unfurnished, uncarpeted north rooms, without fireplaces, looking into a damp courtyard, with a well and a howling dog. My only bed was a rough deal trestle, my only bedding a straw paliasse, with a single coarse blanket. The only other furniture in the room was a deal chair, and a washing-basin on a tripod. No one was allowed to bring me any hot water; and as the water in my room always froze with the intense cold, I had to break the ice with a brass candlestick, or, if that were taken away, with my wounded hands. If, when I came down in the morning, as was often the case, I was almost speechless from sickness and misery, it was always declared to be 'temper'. I was given 'saur-kraut' to eat because the very smell of it made me sick.

Not even Christmas brought respite.

Of all the miserable days in the year, Christmas was the worst. I regard it with loathing unutterable. The presents were of the quintessence of rubbish which I had to receive from my aunts with outward grace and gratitude. The finding all my usual avocations and interests cleared away. The having to sit for hours and hours pretending to be deeply interested in the six huge volumes of *Foxe's Book of Martyrs*, one of which was always doled out for my sustenance. The being compelled – usually with agonizing chilblains – to walk twice to church eight miles through the snow or piercing marsh winds, and sit for hours in mute anguish of congelation, with one of Uncle Julius' interminable sermons in the afternoon.

Reading this, one can't help wondering what it looked like from the aunt's side: maybe Augustus was a thoroughly spoilt, self-centred precious wimp of a nephew, forever whining and complaining. One also wonders whether Hare's imagination didn't run away with him and whether fantasy wasn't feeding into his revenge. But then he tries to be fair to her:

I would not have anyone suppose that, on looking back through the elucidation of years, I can see no merits in my Aunt Esther Hare. The austerities which she enforced upon my mother with regard to me she fully carried out as regarded herself. She was the Inquisition in person. She probed and analysed herself and the motive of her every action quite as bitterly and mercilessly as she probed and analysed others ... To such of the poor as accepted her absolute authority, Aunt Esther was undoubtedly kind, generous and considerate. To the wife of a curate, who

leant confidingly upon her, she was an unselfish and heroic
nurse, equally judicious and tender, in every crisis of a per-
plexing and dangerous illness. To her own sisters and other
members of her family her heart and home were ever open,
with unvarying affection. To her husband, whom her severe
creed taught her to show the same inflexible obedience she
exacted from others, she was utterly devoted ... But to a
little boy who was, to a certain degree, independent of her,
and who had from the first somewhat resented her interfer-
ence, she knew how to be – oh! she was – most cruel.

News of her death came to Hare some twenty years later,
while he was in Rome in 1864, and he gloated on it grimly. 'She
had been carried off by a violent cold which she caught when
lying for hours, in pouring rain, upon her husband's grave ...
no mental constitution can possibly be imagined more happily
constructed for self-torment than hers.'

George Eliot remembered her gaggle of maternal aunts with
a little more affectionate understanding when she painted their
group portrait in the drily amusing sixth chapter of her novel
The Mill on the Floss, set in the rural Midlands among the
lower-middle class before the dead hand of Evangelicalism had
exerted its grip on the Church of England. The four Dodson
sisters grew up with a high sense of their own respectability.
'There was in this family a peculiar tradition as to what was the
right thing in household management and social demeanour,
and the only bitter circumstances attending this superiority
was a painful inability to approve the condiments or the conduct of families ungoverned by the Dodson tradition.' But
within this squadron, Mrs Glegg and Mrs Pullet, the two

daughters who had married 'up', lord it over Mrs Deane and
Mrs Tulliver, who had remained merely respectable, and when
the four sisters gather en masse for an Easter lunch at the Tul-
livers' mill, the Tulliver children, the tousled, rumbustious
Maggie and Tom, rebel in the face of a copybook demonstra-
tion of how aunts should *not* behave.

'Heyday,' said aunt Glegg, with loud emphasis. 'Do little
boys and gells come into a room without taking notice o'
their uncles and aunts? That wasn't the way when *I* was a
little gell.'

'Go and speak to your aunts and uncles, my dears,' said
Mrs Tulliver, looking anxious and melancholy. She wanted
to whisper to Maggie a command to go and have her hair
brushed.

'Well, and how do you do? And I hope you're good children, are you?' said aunt Glegg in the same loud emphatic
way, as she took their hands, hurting them with her large
rings, and kissing their cheeks much against their desire.
'Look up, Tom, look up. Boys as go to boarding school
should hold their heads up. Look at me now.' Tom
declined that pleasure apparently, for he tried to draw his
hand away. 'Put your hair behind your ears, Maggie, and
keep your frock on your shoulder.'

Aunt Glegg always spoke to them in this loud emphatic
way, as if she considered them dead, or perhaps rather idiotic; it was a means, she thought, of making them feel that they
were accountable creatures, and might be a salutary check on
naughty tendencies. Bessy's children were so spoiled –
they'd need have somebody to make them feel their duty.

'Well, my dears,' said aunt Pullet in a compassionate
voice, 'you grow wonderful fast. I doubt they'll outgrow
their strength,' she added, looking over their heads with a
melancholy expression at their mother. 'I think the gell has
too much hair. I'd have it thinned and cut shorter, sister, if I
was you: it isn't good for her health. It's that as makes her
skin so brown, I shouldn't wonder. Don't you think so, sister Deane?'

'I can't say, I'm sure, sister,' said Mrs Deane shutting her
lips close again and looking at Maggie with a critical eye.

'No, no,' said Mr Tulliver, 'the child's healthy enough –
there's nothing ails her. There's red wheat as well as white,
for that matter, and some like the dark grain best. But it 'ud
be as well if Bessy gave the child's hair cut, so as it 'ud lie
smooth.'

In one of those despairing rages that every sensitive child
must endure, Maggie rushes to her room and shears off her
hair. When hunger forces her downstairs to rejoin the family,
her bizarre appearance causes a sensation.

'Fie, for shame,' said aunt Glegg, in her loudest, severest
tone of reproof. 'Little gells as cut their own hair should be
whipped and fed on bread and water – not come and sit
down with their aunts and uncles.'

'Ay, ay,' said uncle Glegg, meaning to give a playful turn
to this denunciation, 'she must be sent to jail, I think, and
they'll cut the rest of her hair off there, and make it all even.'

'She's more like a gypsy nor ever,' said aunt Pullet in a
pitying tone . . .

Maggie's father takes her side when she bursts out sobbing, but the aunts are unmoved. 'How your husband does spoil that child, Bessy,' says Mrs Glegg, in a loud 'aside' to Mrs Tulliver. 'It'll be the ruin of her if you don't take care. *My* father niver brought his children up so, else we should ha' been a different sort of family to what we are.'

For all their shortcomings, the Dodson sisters are solidly rooted in reality; they are married, have children and function as ordinary members of society. Spinster sisters tend to live together and turn inwards, losing their grip on their sanity – not so much damned bad aunts as damned mad aunts, consumed by rituals and obsessions.

Brian Friel's play *Dancing at Lughnasa*, set in rural Donegal in the 1930s, is a poignant tribute to his unmarried mother and his four aunts whose only escape from drudgery and disappointment is a collective explosion of Dionysiac revelry, inspired by songs broadcast on the wireless. Norman Lewis's autobiography *Jackdaw Cake* tells of his orphaned childhood in the hands of three even more wretched aunts: Aunt Polly, an epileptic subject to fits, who daily staged 'an unconscious drama, when she rushed screaming from room to room, sometimes bloodied by a fall'; Aunt Annie, who loved dressing up sometimes as Queen Mary, sometimes as a female Cossack, a pirate or a Spanish dancer; and sorrowful Aunt Li, who had not spoken to Polly for years, only transmitting messages to her via Annie. Every week they met to make a rich fruitcake for the jackdaws that flocked to their garden.

Each aunt took it in turns to bake and ice the cake and to decorate the icing. While they were kept busy doing this

they seemed to me quite changed. Annie wore an ordinary
dress and stopped laughing, Li ceased to cry and Polly's
fits were quieter than on any other day. While the one
whose turn it was did the baking, the others stood about in
the kitchen and watched, and they were as easy to talk to as
at other times they were not.

On Saturday mornings at ten o'clock the cake was fed to
the jackdaws. This had been happening for years, so that
by half past nine the garden was full of birds, anything up
to a hundred of them balancing and swinging with a
tremendous gleeful outcry on the bushes and the low
boughs of the trees. This was the great moment of the week
for my aunts, and therefore for me. The cake would be cut
into three sections and placed on separate plates on the
kitchen table, and then at ten the kitchen windows were
flung wide to admit the great black cataract of birds. For
some hours after this weekly event the atmosphere was one
of calm and contentment, and then the laughter and weeping would start again.

Damned bad, damned mad or maybe simply damned –
aunts are sometimes not so much predators as victims, the
object of a desire for their money which leads those who pursue it to extreme measures. The theme was a staple of mid-
twentieth-century crime fiction, stylishly twisted in Richard
Hull's *The Murder of My Aunt* (1934), in which the narrator,
forced to live alone with his stingy aunt in dreary rural seclusion, records in his diary his development of a fail-safe scheme
to kill her by arranging for her car to crash. The surprise comes
when the aunt suddenly takes over the story: it turns out that

she has been reading her nephew's diary and tracking his every move, so she has dispatched him with an even nastier plot of her own. The joke of the prim maiden aunt who turns out to be a ruthless murderer is also played in Joseph Kesselring's play and film *Arsenic and Old Lace* (1944) and John Newton Chance's *Aunt Miranda's Murder* (1951).

But these fictions seem very tame compared with the appalling real-life aunt-murder stories that pepper newspapers all over the world. In a suburb of Chicago, James Zoph, thirty-eight, battered his frail and disabled Aunt Wanda to death, her face marked by the imprint of his shoes. Zoph's only defence was that he felt he had been cheated out of a $1,000 inheritance. In Sydney, twenty-year-old Richard Cleverly strangled his forty-two-year-old Aunt Susan to death in the expectation of inheriting money she had left him in her will. In Kentucky, the corpse of Ann Branson, eighty-five, was discovered brutally stabbed and bludgeoned. An astute and successful business-woman with a portfolio of rental properties, she had been lending her sweet-talking nephew Russell Winstead, a compulsive gambler, substantial amounts of money. Two days before her death, her ledgers recorded that she had received a cheque from Winstead reimbursing her for $12,000. Ann's records, according to the *America's Most Wanted* website, 'showed that she intended to deposit that check on Monday when the banks reopened. Cops say that if Ann had lived to deposit that check it would have bounced as high as a kangaroo in a moon bounce. As it was, the check was nowhere to be found.' Winstead served as a pallbearer at her funeral; two years later, he was arrested in Costa Rica and at the time of writing awaits trial.

The *Guardian* of 26 August 2004 carried an interview with Susan May, then sixty, who was convicted in 1992 of the murder of her blind eighty-nine-year-old Aunt Hilda. May had lived her entire life in a village in Lancashire. When her mother and aunt became elderly, she gave up her hairdressing salon to care for them, visiting her aunt several times a day to cook, clean and attend to her needs. Hilda was good-natured and cheerful, and nobody knew of any animosity between them. One morning, May arrived to find her aunt dead in bed, having been severely battered. Cupboard doors had been opened, but nothing appeared to be missing. Everyone's assumption was that she had died as the result of an attack by a burglar, and May readily co-operated with the detectives, explaining that as a result of her daily visits and cleaning, her fingerprints would appear all over the house.

Her subsequent arrest left her so incredulous that she engaged only a local solicitor who had never represented anyone accused of murder and who called only two defence witnesses against the prosecution's sixty. She was found guilty on the strength of evidence linking her fingerprints to what appeared to be a trace of her aunt's blood and village gossip that her motive may have been the need to get hold of her aunt's money in order to buy expensive gifts for her 'toyboy' lover. May denies this, pointing out that her aunt was always openly generous with money and there would have been no need to resort to murder – least of all on her mother's birthday.

After two appeals failed, the forensic evidence was called into severe doubt by researchers at the University of Paisley. In April 2005, May was released from prison and is now fighting on to clear her name, supported by a petition signed by over seventy MPs and twenty-five members of the House of Lords, including John Redwood, Tony Benn and the Bishop of Durham.

But there is no possibility of redemption for Baroness de Stempel, who has vanished from the public gaze since her release from prison in 1997, having served seven years for defrauding her aunt. The story is a complex one, involving a horde of missing gold bars and another unresolved murder. Given its cast list of titled people with extremely unsavoury morals, it is not surprising that the case became the subject of enormous media interest and several full-length books.

When she was a child, Susan Wilberforce was closer to her gentle, generous Aunt Puss than to her own mother – Aunt Puss being Lady Illingworth, a wealthy widow who lived in Grosvenor Square. Susan first married a ditheringly hopeless architect, Simon Dale, with whom she had two children, Sophia and Marcus. After they divorced, Susan married the raffish Baron de Stempel, whose financial position was precarious. When Aunt Puss began to sink into senility, the newly ennobled Baroness decided to sort out the problem by hurrying her inheritance up. Colluding to some extent with her children, she forged a revision of her aunt's will favourable to herself. Then, in 1984, after claiming to the authorities that Lady Illingworth was an uncontrollable alcoholic and embarrassing sex maniac, De Stempel arranged for her to be confined in a state-run old people's home near Hereford, where she was left to moulder on supplementary benefit. When she died two years later, no announcement was made and no member of the family attended her funeral, the bill for which remained unpaid. The body was cremated, despite Lady Illingworth's clear wishes as a devout Catholic that she should be buried alongside her beloved husband in the family vault.

Meanwhile, via a total of sixty-seven forgeries, Susan de Stempel had been engineering a massive purloining of Aunt Puss's assets: forty-seven vanloads of her possessions were taken from the house in Grosvenor Square and her cash was squirrelled away into forty-nine fraudulent bank accounts. What happened to her thirty gold bars, worth £12 million at 1990 prices, has never been established.

A year after Lady Illingworth's death, Simon Dale was found murdered. Baroness de Stempel, who loathed her ex-husband, was arrested, tried and acquitted. No motive for this apparently pointless crime has ever emerged, and it remains possible that it was the result of a bizarre case of mistaken identity. But De Stempel was rumbled, and a year later she was back in court, where she pleaded guilty to forgery and theft. 'Your treatment of Lady Illingworth was absolutely barbarous,' the judge told her at sentencing. 'Having taken all her money you cast her off . . . she went to an old people's home, but you allowed her to go there as a pauper. It was a truly wicked thing to do.'

Visited in prison by the crime reporter Terry Kirby, author of *The Trials of the Baroness*, Baroness de Stempel remained haughty and dismissive, claiming that people simply didn't understand the way that aristocrats went about these matters and that she was only taking what would in any case have become hers after her aunt died. Kirby also noted 'her habit of uttering an almost silent laugh, so that when she tilts her head back and opens her mouth slightly and smiles, only a faintly audible sound emerges'.

Auntie

(Maynard Dakin, 1911)

Auntie, Auntie, you're always up to date
I've often wondered why you've never tried the
  marriage state,
You eligible bachelors who're looking for a mate
Try Auntie – dear Auntie.
Auntie, Auntie, you've got a wicked eye,
A marvellous attraction to the man who's pass-
  ing by,
And when he leaves his happy home,
And people wonder why
It's Auntie – all Auntie.

Auntie, Auntie, she's always right on top,
She's a 'goer' and she knows it, and
She doesn't mean to stop
She takes the bun – the biscuit – in fact, the
  baker's shop
Does Auntie – dear Auntie.

8

Fairy-Tale Aunts

Until the eighteenth century, nobody gave their aunt a second thought – or at least that's the impression that the written record leaves. Aunts don't figure with any potency or vividness in the Bible or classical mythologies. Stith Thompson's epic survey of the themes and motifs in folk cultures records very few auntly appearances, and even those are only peripheral or incidental. Bogeymen and stepmothers abound in children's stories, but there are no aunts of any significance in the fairy tales of Perrault, Grimm or Hans Christian Andersen. On the subject of aunts *The Oxford Dictionary of Nursery Rhymes* records only this riddle, dating from 1630:

> There were three sisters in a hall
> There came a knight amongst them all;
> Good morrow, aunt, to the one,
> Good morrow, aunt, to the other,
> Good morrow, gentlewoman, to the third,
> If you were aunt,
> As the other two be
> I would say good morrow
> Then, aunts, all three.

This dearth of mythical aunts may surprise us, inasmuch as aunts feature so prominently in modern children's literature that we have come to think of them as a basic ingredient of fantasy – specifically, of the phenomenon described by psycho-analysis as 'the family romance', in which (according to Bruno Bettelheim) children are seized by 'the idea that one's parents are not really one's parents, but that one is the child of some exalted personage, and that, due to unfortunate circumstances, one has been reduced to living with these people, who claim to be one's parents. These daydreams take various forms; often only one parent is thought to be a false one – which parallels a frequent situation in fairy-tales, where one parent is the real one, the other a step-parent.'

Yet for millennia aunts somehow succeeded in sidestepping this Oedipal drama. Instead of replacing a mother, they supplement her: an aunt is a reassuring rather than disruptive figure, representing security and stability, patience and wisdom, reflective of the secondary meaning of the word 'aunt' as any familiar and benevolent elderly lady in one's community. The literary function of aunts was to collect stories, rhymes and homilies and provide disinterested advice on life, as in Mrs Pilkington's *The Calendar* (1807), 'chiefly consisting of dialogues between an aunt and her nieces designed to inspire the juvenile mind with a love of virtue and the study of nature'. These conversations were evidently written by someone with no sense of humour, and one can imagine Jane Austen being vastly amused by their Mr Collins-ish heavy-handed pomposity.

'I was in Herefordshire, you know, aunt,' said Louisa, 'last September, and all the apples were gathered whilst I was there.'

'I do not doubt it, my dear,' replied Mrs Manderville, 'because they do not let them hang to be completely ripe, for they are always laid together in large heaps to ripen before they are taken to the mill.'

'What, do they make flour of apples?' exclaimed the unreflecting Eliza.

'I am rejoiced no stranger heard you make such a ridiculous enquiry. Let me intreat you never to speak without reflecting, or you will be thought an absolute idiot, my dear,' replied Mrs Manderville.

Sententious tosh of this sort is something that many evangelizing Christian lady authors spouted when they wrote improving books for the young. Describing themselves as Aunt Such-and-Such guaranteed a tone of friendly familiarity: taking the 1850s–1870s alone, the library catalogues list new pamphlets, tracts and anthologies by Aunt Agnes, Aunt Fanny, Aunt Louisa, Aunt Mavor, Aunt Mary and Aunt Mildred. Charlotte M. Yonge became Aunt Charlotte when she published her *Stories of English History*, *Evenings at Home with the Poets* and *Scripture Readings*; and in the US, Sarah Schoonmaker Baker took the pseudonym of Aunt Friendly for her pioneering teenage novels *The Boy Friend*, *The Children on the Plains* and *The Jewish Twins*.

But at about the same time that these books appeared, the aunt suddenly develops a more definite fictional personality of her own. To establish why this happened, you could delve deeply into the conflicting theories proposed by anthropologists, sociologists and historians about the rise and fall, or the fall and rise, or the persistence or non-existence of the nuclear family and the extended family in industrial societies, but you would probably not resurface much enlightened. Perhaps it is better just to accept that the later Victorians found the notion of the bloodline aunt very interesting and amusing.

Take, for instance, *Aunt Atta*, a children's novel published anonymously in 1872. It opens with Johnny, Edmund, Lizzy and Charlotte Arden smugly congratulating themselves that they have only sensible married aunts who present no problems. 'We haven't got a tiresome cross thing like Carby-Maxwell's aunt to be always teasing and scolding us,' says Johnny. 'Ugh! I'd rather have a little black boy . . . Tommy Broughton said it was because they were such nasty, cross, ugly old things that nobody would marry them.'

The Ardens' father then reveals the imminent arrival of the spinster Aunt Esther, her existence previously unsuspected (this is a persistent theme in literature about aunts: they are often an unknown quantity of unknown provenance, arriving suddenly or unexpectedly and disrupting or transforming a settled family unit; see p. 129). The children gloomily anticipate 'a stiff puked-up thing', but are very surprised when what appears is 'a very little person' with 'a small good-tempered face', 'very white teeth, large bright eyes' and 'a merry sweet voice'. Her enlightening effect on the household is miraculous. 'I have very often been called Pussy, only think of that,' she tells the children, but mercifully they prefer to call her Atta. Baby Tiny soon pipes up, 'Of all me aunts, me do like me Aunt Atta de best.'

The ensuing plot is virtually non-existent, beyond repeatedly demonstrating Aunt Atta's benign moral influence over her nieces and nephews – 'She was very kind indeed to them, and was always ready to do anything that was right to please them, but she did not allow them to be troublesome, or ask over and over again for what was once refused them.' This paragon is one of the first of many such aunts to inhabit English children's literature: the slightly mysterious visitant who turns out to be much nicer than expected.

American children's literature of this period is almost obsessively interested in the sentimental theme of the orphan child sent to live with an aunt. Literary critics trace this to the success of Elizabeth Wetherell's *The Wide, Wide World*, published in 1850, in which the ardent and impulsive thirteen-year-old Ellen gradually softens the heart of frosty and flinty, spick-and-span Aunt Fortune. The same situation recurs many times in books of the era: in Kate Douglas Wiggin's *Rebecca of Sunnybrook Farm*, for example, where the eponymous heroine is sent to live with 'conscientious, economical, industrious' Aunt Miranda; or in Susan Coolidge's *What Katy Did*, where the 'very neat and particular' Aunt Izzie finally reveals 'a warm heart hidden under her fidgety ways'; or in Eleanor H. Porter's *Pollyanna* (1913), where a starchy spinster takes responsibility for her orphaned niece out of a sense of duty rather than affection but finds herself ultimately disarmed by Pollyanna's 'glad game' of finding 'a silver lining in every cloud'.

Boys have aunts too, notably Mark Twain's Tom Sawyer, whose Aunt Polly is powerless before his charm. 'Laws-a-me!' she wails. 'He's my own dead sister's boy, poor thing, and I ain't got the heart to lash him somehow.' But she remains a flat, unexplored personality who plays no real part in the novel, similar to Dorothy's undescribed Aunt Em in L. Frank Baum's *The Wizard of Oz*. (More psychologically authentic is the relationship that Tom's friend, the genuine outsider Huckleberry Finn, doesn't have with the Widow Douglas: 'she took me for her son,' he tells the reader, 'and allowed she would sivilize me; but it was rough living in the house all the time, considering how dismal regular and decent the widow was in all her ways; and so when I couldn't stand it no longer, I lit out.')

Louisa May Alcott tried a bit harder. An enthusiastic aunt herself, she was much influenced in childhood by the stories told her by her own, rather grand great-aunt, who had known Martha Washington and General Lafayette. Perhaps she contributed to the figure of the lame, grouchy and wealthy Aunt March in *Little Women,* to whom Jo, Beth, Amy and Meg, living in reduced circumstances, are unfortunately beholden in expectations of inheritance. A later and lesser known novel of Alcott's, *Eight Cousins, or The Aunt-Hill*, presents Rose, yet another orphan who is taken in and fussed over by six maiden aunts, their personalities ranging from the pious and lugubrious Aunt Myra to the 'truly beautiful old maiden' Aunt Peace, 'an adviser, confidante and friend'. Although these ladies are sympathetically treated in the novel, it is the male influence of Uncle Alec, a sexy doctor, which helps her to grow up strong and sensible.

In twentieth-century children's literature, aunts learn to be callous and even hostile. There's stingy, bad-tempered Aunt Sally, a figure in Barbara Euphan Todd's *Worzel Gummidge*, popular as a radio and television series dating back to 1935. A curious tale written and illustrated in 1937 by Edward Ardizzone called *Lucy Brown and Mr Grimes* tells of the orphan Lucy, living with an aunt 'who was very busy and could not be bothered with her very much' (is she drawn on Aunt Dete, in Johanna Spyri's *Heidi*, who dumps the eponymous five-year-

old orphan on her grandfather?). One day, while walking alone in the park, Lucy meets an old man who invites her to tea. He is called Mr Grimes, and her aunt allows her to accept the invitation 'as she had heard that [he] was very respectable'. Lucy has a lovely time talking to this elderly gentleman, who eventually writes to her aunt to ask if he could adopt Lucy and take her to live with him in the country. How times change: the preoccupied aunt expresses no objection to this arrangement, which nowadays would attract the attention of every child protection unit in the land.

Enid Blyton's aunts are entirely without interest. The Famous Five's Aunt Fanny, married to the splenetic absent-minded scientist Uncle Quentin ('a very clever man, but rather frightening') seems good for nothing except providing the wretched adventure-prone band with full English breakfasts, packed lunches, cream teas and lashings of ginger pop and ham sandwiches. Her American equivalent is the widowed Aunt May in the *Spiderman* comics, a kindly, over-worked, genteelly impoverished domestic mule whose only active dramatic function is to provide the orphaned Peter Parker with regular meals, a roof over his head and someone to protect from the forces of evil.

It is in the annals of Richmal Crompton's much more engaging hero William Brown that the aunt comes into her own as a comic figure generally representative of outmoded proprieties against which William anarchically struggles to assert himself. In almost all of the thirty-eight *Just William* books, written between 1922 and 1970, an aunt makes an appearance. Crompton herself was unmarried and once described herself 'as probably the last surviving example of the Victorian professional aunt', drawing inspiration for her hero's derring-do from a scallywag younger brother (and presumably Tom Sawyer as well). 'Aunty Ray', as she was called, was naturally playful and adored fooling around with her nieces and nephews – one of them remembered her nobly volunteering to sit in the garden shed and play the role of General Custer at his last stand.

William's aunts are not such good sports. He seems to have hundreds of them, though over the decades their traits seem to melt into one another. First comes Aunt Jane, 'tall and prim and what she called "house proud"', the vice-president of something suspicious called the New Era Society. Is she the same person as Great-Aunt Jane, 'tall and angular and precise' and a member of the Plymouth Brethren? William attends what appears to be the latter's deathbed, at which he starts an unseemly scuffle with his golden-curled cousin Francis. Great-Aunt Jane is roused by the noise and unexpectedly takes

William's side – 'Go for it, William,' she shouts, 'get one in on his nose.' This aggressive old lady later takes William to the fair, where she starts hurling coconuts and taking repeated rides on the helter-skelter.

But Jane is as good as William's aunts get. Aunt Ellen is a terrible bore, Aunt Lilian merely attends to grandfather. Fat and pompous Aunt Emily snores so loudly that William charges his friends a penny a time to witness the hilarious spectacle of her slumbers. Aunt Emma gives him a book of church history for Christmas. Great-Aunt Augusta tells him that 'there's no joy like the joy of duty done'. Then there's Aunt Belle, Aunt Evangelina, Aunt Florence, Aunt Flossie, Aunt Hester, Aunt Julia, Aunt Louie, Aunt Lucy, Aunt Maggie and old Aunt Susan Cobleigh and all, none of them clearly defined. Other members of William's gang the Outlaws are similarly plagued: his closest chum Ginger has Aunt Arabelle, 'a small short-sighted woman with ink-stained fingers and untidy hair' who scribbles away as an Agony Aunt for *Woman's Sphere*, and Aunt Amelia, a fanatic gardener who lives with a Sapphic 'literary friend called Flavia'.

Because they can be kept at a distance, William's aunts never become truly threatening; they are simply another thwarting irritant sent out by the adult world, to be swatted, outsmarted or evaded. They even have their uses (presents and monetary tips), and in the 1950s, William's spiritual cousin Nigel Molesworth finds a patch of indulgence for them in a corner of his otherwise hard heart. 'Aunts are not bad but they are inclined to be soppy and call you darling chiz chiz chiz,' he reports in *How to Be Topp*, Geoffrey Willans' classic account of life from the perspective of a cynical prep-school boy. 'Also you are just like your mater or your pater whichever happen to be the plainer. Aunts ask you how you are getting on at skool and you say o all right may you be forgiven.'

But something very unpleasant happens to aunts when they are drawn into the violent and heartless world of Roald Dahl. In *James and the Giant Peach* (1967), they become evil grotesques drawn on Cinderella's ugly sisters. James is orphaned after his parents are eaten by a rhinoceros, and he is sent to live with two 'really horrible' aunts, Sponge and Spiker. Sponge is fat and short with piggy eyes and is reminiscent of 'a great white soggy over-boiled cabbage'. Spiker is lean and tall and bony, with 'a screeching voice and long wet narrow lips'. They call innocent James 'selfish and lazy and cruel' and 'the disgusting little beast' and never let him out of their 'queer ramshackle house'. Fortunately, the Giant Peach which rescues James from his incarceration rolls over them, leaving them ironed out flat, dead and unredeemed.

These coarse caricatures are imitated by J. K. Rowling in her *Harry Potter* cycle. The orphaned Harry is lodged with his late mother's hysterical sister Aunt Petunia, a vicious termagant who bullies and humiliates Harry in favour of her fat and disagreeable son. Her husband Vernon has a sister, Aunt Marge, who comes to visit in *Harry Potter and the Prisoner of Azkaban*. 'Huge, beefy and purple-faced', with a moustache and a bulldog, Marge is so pompous and infuriating that Harry illicitly draws on his magic powers to inflate her like a balloon and send her floating up to the ceiling.

Such revenge fantasies are not very edifying. They are enjoyed precisely because that's what they are, but the sad effect is to leave children regarding their aunts not as possible allies so much as paper-tiger authority figures, waiting to be mocked and shot down. A more subtle and endearing treatment of auntly adoption is provided by Eva Ibbotson's *Island of the Aunts* (1999), a delightfully imaginative novel which takes the spite out of Dahlian excess. 'Kidnapping children is not a good idea,' runs its opening line. 'All the same, sometimes it has to be done.' Aunts Etta, Coral and Myrtle are aunts without satisfactory nieces or nephews. The three middle-aged ladies live on a desert island with their centenarian father and prophetic cousin Sybil. As eco-conscious guardians of the exotic fauna and flora, they are in need of fresh blood and help from open-minded youngsters – hence the kidnapping scheme.

They return to England to find suitable victims and invent an agency, Unusual Aunts (see p. 199). Aunt Etta, who does 'fifty press-ups before breakfast' and has 'a small but not at all unpleasant moustache on her upper lip', is sent to King's Cross station with the assignment of escorting Minette, an unhappy child who is being shuffled between neglectful divorced parents in London and Edinburgh. Arty Aunt Coral takes charge of Fabio, a half-English, half-Brazilian boy whose snobbish grandparents are sending him back to a boarding school he detests. Ditsy Aunt Myrtle mistakenly lands up with a spoilt American brat, Lambert.

The three children are whisked back to the desert island, where the aunts provide Minette and Fabio with an education in wonder. They are put to work milking goats, feeding seals and de-oiling birds, and they meet mermaids, dragons and friendly monsters. Soon they grow to love the place, the aunts and their labours; Lambert, however, just whines and plots his escape with the help of his dratted mobile phone. The climax comes when the legendary kraken wakes in the sea, transforming nature with his healing hum.

Back in London, the police are alerted to the disappearances and newspaper headlines proclaim that AUNT PLAGUE MENACES THE CITY. 'There was talk in parliament of a curfew for aunts, forcing them to be in bed by eight o'clock; the *Daily Echo* said that aunts should be electronically tagged.' Eventually, through Lambert's conniving, the children are 'rescued' and the aunts charged with kidnapping. Aunt Myrtle escapes prosecution because Lambert's father is too lunatic and paranoid to press charges. In court, Minette and Fabio announce that Etta and Coral had chosen, not kidnapped them, and that they were not detained either by force or for ransom. The aunts are let off and bequeath the children the magic island in their will.

Etta, Coral and Myrtle are typical of the modern aunt in children's books. They continue to represent a moral influence, but not one relating to everyday notions of good behaviour. Instead they are liberators, opening conventional childhoods up to the adventure of eccentricity. In Madeleine L'Engle's science-fiction quest novel *A Wrinkle in Time*, the paralysed heroine Meg is nursed back to health on the planet Ixchel by Aunt Beast, a tentacular monster with no hair or eyes but the warmest of hearts. Paddington Bear's Aunt Lucy pays for an inflatable dinghy with accumulated postal orders. Dee Shulman's Aunt Belle, a throwback to Auntie Mame (see p. 121), is a glamorous author and sometime film star infatuated with her Abyssinian cat. Mina Taylor's Aunt Lizzie buys a lion from a defunct circus. Jo Pestum's Aunt Thea drives an antediluvian

Tin Lizzie, which she starts with a crank handle. She is the size of 'a light heavyweight boxer' and wears 'a caftan like a woolly dressing gown one side and a hairless sealskin the other'. Roy Apps's Barmy Aunt Boomerang has a dog called Smith-Taylor and dresses 'up to the nines, with so many earrings, bracelets and scarves dangling from various parts of her body that she looked like a Christmas tree'. 'She was crazy,' concludes the child narrator. 'But she was different.'

In an era in which a massified corporate culture cynically hard-sells children an ever narrower range of options, products and models, aunts such as these show the way to a simpler yet richer world which celebrates the freedom to be crazy but different – in other words, yourself.

Aunt Maggie's Remedy

(George Formby, reinterpreted by Lonnie Donegan)

It's me Auntie Maggie's home-made remedy
Guaranteed never to fail
Now that's the stuff that will do the trick
It's sold at every chemist for one and a kick.

Now if you get lumbago, rheumatics or gout
Or a pain in your Robert E. Lee,
Don't kick up a shindy
You'll never get windy
With Auntie Maggie's remedy.

Now I know a girl who is putting on weight
In a spot where it just shouldn't be
So I said to Nelly
Now rub your *knee-cap*
With Auntie Maggie's remedy.

9

Bargain Aunts

For Americans, the idea of an aunt as 'any benevolent practical woman who exercises these qualities to the benefit of her circle of acquaintances' has been more persistent than it is in Britain, and this may explain the widespread commercial exploitation of the word and its association with home-spun, home-grown, home-cooked goods you can trust.

An auntly product will treat, not cheat, you: solidly and traditionally made, it is more concerned with old-fashioned substance than new-fangled style. Tried and tested in the kitchen rather than the factory, it is suitable for universal family consumption. Like 'community' and 'organic', 'aunt' has no adverse connotation.

The most celebrated auntly product in the US – on a par with Betty Crocker and Ronald McDonald – is Aunt Jemima's Pancake Mix (nowadays Pancake and Waffle Mix and owned by the Pepsi corporation). This stuff has an interesting history. It was launched by the Pearl Milling Company in 1889 and named after a popular vaudeville song of the day. The picture on the packet depicted a Southern mammy – drawn, in fact, from an African-American woman from Chicago called Nancy Green, who became the very stereotype of the loyal and cheerful black servant – wearing a broad smile and a bandanna round her head. 'Honey, it's easy to be de sweetheart o you' family,' read the advertising copy. 'Yo' know how de men folks an' de

young folks all loves my tasty pan-
cakes. An yo' can make dem fo'
dem jiffy-quick, an' jus' right
every time, wid my magic
ready-mix.'

Nancy Green demon-
strated this early conve-
nience food (dried milk
the secret ingredient) in
person at the Chicago
World's Fair of 1893,
causing such a sensation
that the police had to be
called in to control the crowds.
Dressed as Aunt Jemima, she continued to tour the country for the next
thirty years promoting the mix, which was bought out in 1925
by Quaker Oats.

With the advent of civil rights in the 1960s, the image of
Aunt Jemima began to be perceived as insultingly servile, and
she was redrawn slimmer and younger. In 1989, she was given
a complete makeover and made into an 'aspirational' buppie
(black upwardly mobile professional), losing the stigma of the
bandanna and given a fashionable coiffure, pearl earrings and a
lacy collar instead.

A trawl by Google reveals many other American auntly products, divided into three categories:

Crafts and antiques
Aunt Billie's Unique Handmade Gifts
Aunt Flossie's Attic
Aunt Annie's Crafts
Aunt Helen's Handicrafts
Aunt Mary's Yarns
Auntie Em's Dollhouses and Accessories
Aunt Lois' Homemade Soap
Aunt Judy's Attic
Aunt Sue's Country Corner
Aunt Jane's Country Store
Aunt Joy's Personalised Christmas Stockings
Aunt Annie's Quilt Nook
Auntie's Homespun Crafts
Aunt Emma's Homesteader's Connection Emporium

Prepared foods and recipes
Aunt Lynnie's Kitchen
Aunt Libby's Kitchen
Aunt Edna's Kitchen
Aunt Leah's Fudge
Aunt Clara's Dominican Recipes
Aunt Betty's Steamed Puddings
Aunt Minnie's Southern Style Entrées and Desserts
Aunt Sally's Original Creole Pralines
Aunt Sarah's Kitchen
Auntie Joe's Gourmet Gift Baskets

Aunt Selma's Chocolates
Aunt Ellie's Borscht
Aunt Ruby's Peanuts
Aunt Nellie's Pickled Beets
Aunt Wanda's Turkey Carcass Soup
Aunt Lizzie's Gourmet Cheese Straws
Aunt Gussie's Country Delectables
Aunt Viola's Best Doggone Caesar Dressing
Aunt Jem's Home Made Frozen Raw Pet Food
Auntie Anne's Pretzels

Bed and breakfast
Aunt Sadie's, the Ozarks
Aunt Olly's, Rhode Island
Aunt Suzie's, Pennsylvania
Aunt Martha's, Florida
Auntie's House, Amarillo
Aunt Daisie's, Illinois
Aunt Rebecca's, Baltimore
Aunt Peg's, St Augustine
Aunt Irma's, Ohio

Cynical Europeans don't buy into the auntly guarantee of quality with the same fervour as the Americans. In Germany, a Tante Paula is a form of motorized scooter – why was it so named, one wonders? – but apart from a scattering of restaurants called Tante this or that, the idea of the aunt is not a big selling point. Except perhaps in Belfast, where Aunt Mollie's Quality Foods produce crumble mixture and ready-rolled pastry (puff and shortcrust) and Aunt Sandra's Candy Factory is a little patch of sweetie heaven, all humbugs and honey-comb, lollies, fudge and toffee apples. Almost all these aunts are, of course, mere figments of an ad man's imagination, but Aunt Sandra has a corporeal existence: she established the factory in 1953 and has now handed it over to her nephew David Moore.

In Britain, the most celebrated branding of the aunt comes in the shape of a pioneering employment agency which made its reputation on the strength of its impeccable gentility and respectability. This was the brainchild of Gertrude Maclean, a scion of a large Edwardian clan whose seven brothers and sisters were scattered in commanding positions over the pink areas of the globe. Gertrude was the one who stayed at home, unable to bag a husband amid the terrible dearth of young men that followed the carnage of the First World War. Meanwhile, her siblings bundled their offspring back to England to be educated, and Gertrude's role was to pick them up from ports and railway stations, deliver them to schools and look after them in the holidays. She was an ace aunt, by all accounts, 'a rock and a sport', playful and affectionate, and as her nieces and nephews all began to outgrow her, she decided in 1921 to continue her activities on a commercial basis and establish a business she called 'Universal Aunts'.

Her timing was perfect. War had put an end to the bottom-less pool of residential domestic servants. Women may have had less chance of marrying, but they now had the vote, their first MP, more chance of entering the professions – and shorter skirts and fewer corsets. It became not only respectable but also economically necessary for the middle class of unmarried or widowed women to seek remunerative work, so long as it wasn't demeaningly physical. To be a Universal Aunt was to be at once useful and independent without losing caste.

The advertisement in *The Times* read:

UNIVERSAL AUNTS
(LADIES OF IRREPROACHABLE BACKGROUND)
CARE OF CHILDREN
CHAPERONAGE
HOUSE FURNISHING
SHOPPING FOR THE COLONIES
RESEARCH WORK

Working out of a tiny room off Sloane Street in the mornings and conducting interviews on sofas in Harrods' Ladies' Rest Room in the afternoons, Gertrude Maclean (under the *nom de guerre* of Miss Safrana Fort) offered to do 'anything for anyone at any time' – short of prostitution or marriage brokering – at a fee of 7s. 6d. for the first hour and 5s. thereafter (the aunts themselves were paid 3s. per hour). Most of her clients required escorts ('proxy parents') for their children, but advice on interior decoration and How to Get On in Society were also much in demand.

There was no shortage of labour, with notes kept on all applicants. For example:

MISS ELIZABETH PRATT-STEED
Disciplinarian. Firm without being brutal. Can converse on physics, spiritualism or foreign missions. Not a time-waster, good cheap aunt.

MISS PHYLLIS BECKETT

Young and sporty. Knows all about 'footer' and white mice. Can slide down banisters at a push.

MISS HYACINTH PLUMMER

Thirties (late). Can play Halma, Snakes & Ladders and tell moral stories. No doubt has a selection of modesty vests or chiffon roses for the front of her lower necklines.

MISS CHARLOTTE HEDGECOMBE

Age 55

Hefty, stern, stands no nonsense. Stickler for etiquette and deportment. On Borstal Board of Governors, Zoological Society's certificate. Cope older boys, any number.

Universal Aunts went on to become an imperial institution, claiming on its eightieth anniversary to have employed 'over three quarters of a million men and women and undertaken over a million services'. Even in a Blairite Britain which has devalued its brand of sterling Home Counties reliability, it continues to flourish, taking a pride in discreetly meeting the outlandish requests of oil sheikhs and Russian billionaires without turning a pink-

rinsed hair. Nice country-reared gels, with a practical rather
than intellectual bent and the stamp of finishing school upon
their brains, form the backbone of its staff: in the late 1970s, one
Lady Diana Spencer spent time on its books, working with
children.

Caroline Muir first worked for one of Universal Aunts' imi-
tators, Oxford Aunts. She was preceded there by her mother,
who had just left Caroline's father and desperately needed a
source of income. Having been a deb, she could cook cordon
bleu and throw a party, but she had a good brain too: at forty-
two, she had just obtained an MA in Comparative Literature.
She came down with a bump when she realized the only job
she qualified for was mucking out donkeys on a smallholding
in the Cotswolds owned by an elderly lady with Bloomsbury
connections.

Caroline herself came out of boarding school at seventeen
and saw joining Oxford Aunts as an obvious way to earn some
money. 'They immediately put me on to dons' wives who were
so cantankerous that they kept losing their cleaners,' she
remembers.

*The first one was the widow of the head of Exeter College.
She must have been in her late eighties and she gave me the
newspaper to iron – I'd no idea that this was something that
used to be done quite regularly in the 1930s. She had eleven
old hoovers piled up in the basement – one of them was made
of cast iron, and it occurred to me that it would probably
flatten the newspaper quite effectively.*

*Then came a woman who lived in a sepulchral house in
the Banbury Road. She opened the door and hardly spoke*

except to hand me a toothbrush and say 'skirting boards'. And I said, 'Just the skirting boards? I've been booked from 9 to 11.' And she said, 'Yes, skirting boards.' So I went down on my hands and knees and cleaned the skirting boards with a toothbrush. I had to go very, very slowly, because the job could have taken just five minutes. And it annoyed me that the rest of the house was utterly filthy.

Then I went to London and joined Universal Aunts, and that was very different. Oxford was full of elderly academic ladies who had no interest in anything domestic and had mostly lost their marbles. In London, it was all extremely wealthy people who had just run into a staffing emergency. Here was I, a middle-class Yorkshire girl from a respectable boarding school, flung into the world of the super-rich.

I was sent to a house in Eaton Square, owned by an oil sheikh – he must have been a billionaire. All the food came from that caterer Justin de Blank and they must have thrown away more than they ate. Even the ashtrays were solid gold and the size of frisbees. He'd married this girl who'd advertised Wella hair products – they'd met in Annabel's, I think. She was very beautiful and wore dark glasses indoors, which I thought odd. She had a really broad North Country accent and she wanted to talk. Everything had gone wrong. He had fired the previous cleaner and the cook, and she had just given birth to a second daughter, when he was desperate for a son. Her husband had flown into a rage and started beating her – she had a black eye, hence those dark glasses.

Anyway, she fell on me because my accent was received pronunciation and she asked me if I'd interview the next cook. I was seventeen, in pink dungarees. 'Really, I'm just a cleaner,' I said. So I started on one of the bathrooms and noticed that the shower was full of faeces. I didn't say anything and just tried to deal with it, but well, there was another deposit the next morning, and by the third day, it was getting me down. I began to explain the problem to the wife and she blurted out that it was her husband's bathroom and that nobody else ever used it. Then I told her about the mess and she was appalled, but said she was so terrified of him that she didn't know what to do.

Well, he was simply a pig. I ironed about a dozen shirts for him one day, and when he came into the kitchen and saw the way I'd done them, he just picked the whole pile up and threw them back into the washing machine, screaming that I'd have to start again. But by then I couldn't have cared less. I just thought, 'I'm going to New York, this isn't real life.' It was so poignant. The wife said to me at one point, 'I can't leave him because my children will be taken back to Saudi and I'll never see them again.'

A year or so later the agency sent me to Paris, in a boxy blue suit that Mary Poppins might have found acceptable, to look after the children of a Comtesse who lived in a fabulous vast apartment overlooking Les Invalides. There was a helipad on the roof and a Monet in the drawing room. The idea was that I would speak English to the children – give them English conversation and English manners – and be an aunt to them rather than a nanny; they were very unruly and needed a maternal figure.

Their mother was very depressed. Her sister had committed suicide, she was a great friend of Christina Onassis, and

I don't think she was mentally stable. She used to play the piano all day – I think she was in the early stages of overwhelming grief at losing her sister. She was only in her late twenties, I should think, and yet she couldn't bear to be close to the children. So I was the one who put them to bed and cuddled them.

They were five and three, very young to be full-time at school. The five-year-old boy screamed so loudly on the way to school that he vomited all over the lift. And I stood there thinking, 'This child is as mentally disturbed as his mother and I don't have the special skills you need to look after them.' Then the little girl would say things like, 'I am a countess, my mother is a countess, my aunt was a princess and I'm going to be a princess too when I grow up.' And for once it wasn't just a fantasy: she probably is a princess by now.

I didn't last there very long though, because one night the boy asked me, in his materialistic way, what my favourite thing in all the world was, and I told him it was my Gucci watch – rather hideous actually, but something that my first love had given me. And that night it disappeared – in the morning, it just wasn't there. It's very difficult to say, 'Look, I had this conversation with your son, and now my watch has gone,' but I did and they were furious – not with the boy, but with me for suggesting that he might be responsible. So the mother said to me, 'Is there a problem?' And I said, 'Yes, there is, this is a job for a professional nanny.' So she paid me off and I went to live on a barge and played backgammon.

Recently, I sent a friend to Universal Aunts, because she had just bolted like my mother had. She didn't have her own house, her children had left home and she was totally inse-

cure. The first posting they gave her was an elderly politician who lived in Hampstead. They got on like a house on fire and it restored her confidence – she bought another house, got a divorce and remarried. The politician is a widower in his nineties and is almost blind, but she had a marvellous time with him, taking him off to parties at Downing Street and cooking when Gordon Brown came round to supper. Because he's a socialist and she's half-Italian, half-Welsh and work-ing class, he treats her with total respect – he's terrifically kind to her and she does it all out of love.

But it all ended up rather badly. The other Aunt with whom she shared the job was jealous that she was so favoured by the politician and set about accusing my friend of inappropriate behaviour. All rubbish, but they fired her and my friend proudly stomped off and got a proper job else-where. The old man is very upset and rings her three times a week to ask when she is coming back – he has no idea that she was dumped behind his back. The whole thing is very sad – perhaps she did indeed bounce on a trampoline at his request, but so what, if it made him happy?

I think working as a Universal Aunt is terrific for people who can't quite figure out what the next step is but who are generally good company and positive about life, with practi-cal skills. Universal Aunts should be invisible – they clean up the mess, they produce the gin and tonics and cups of tea, and provide tactful surveillance. You're in a huge position of trust, and it can be very rewarding. It's fascinating to get such an intimate glimpse into people's lives, and hugely sat-isfying to go into an absolute tip and turn it around and sort things out. And so many older people are longing to talk to young people and find out what they are thinking. The nice ones chatted to me a lot and lent me books and gave me advice about the life that I was teetering on the edge of – I was longing to soak up all their wisdom. Some of them were great fun too. So you could say I was not so much a Universal Aunt, more a Universal Niece.

My Aunt's Will

(Joseph Tabrar and Harry Boden, 1903)

My great-grandfather's father had an uncle
And on his nephew's side he had a niece
And that niece had a brother, and his sister had a mother
Who when she died went to rest in peace.
But before she went she made a will and left two thousand
    pounds
And I'm satisfied with everything because
I've proved my father was my uncle, and my mother was
    my aunt
And I'm the same as what I should be if I was.

My great-grandfather's father had an uncle
And his grandfather's father had a niece
When uncle's sister Annie had a nephew and his granny
Was aunt to aunt who went to rest in peace;
But before she died she made a will and left me fifteen
    shillings
But I don't care for that because you see,
I've proved we are, who we are, except those who never
    were
And what is more I've also proved I'm me.

10

The Lunch Club

Angela Woods

There were my real aunts, and then there were my aunties.
Real aunts first. On my mum's side, there was Aunt Daphne,
who was her twin. They were brought up in Lambeth and in
Brighton, and they were very close – they'd been evacuated
together to Somerset during the war. Later they both worked in
Woolworth's and went hopping in Kent.

I was close to Aunt Daphne until I was fifteen, and close to
her daughter, my cousin Susan. I remember we went to
Brighton for a sports day and to Billy Smart's circus on
Clapham Common. Then, as we got older, we just drifted apart.

Daphne only lives a few miles away from me in Morden, but
the last time we saw each other was at my mum's funeral in
2002. There isn't a rift or anything like that. I still send birth-
day and Christmas cards, but since mum died, I find I can't
even bear to hear her voice on the phone. It reminds me of Mum
so vividly, and it's too upsetting.

Dad came from Limerick, and his childhood was almost
identical to what Frank McCourt describes in Angela's Ashes.
He lived in the same parish, and you can almost see his house

*in the film version. He came to London when he was nineteen
and started work on a building site. His background was poor
and very Catholic, but he was bright at school, and if he'd had
the chance, he would have liked to have been a teacher. He's still
working at the age of sixty-nine, for Esher Housing Association.*

*He met Mum when they were both working at Wall's sausage
factory in Lambeth, and they lived in Stockwell and Kennington. They had five children. I'm the oldest, born in 1955.*

*Dad's younger sister, our Aunt Mary, lived with us for a
time. She's very nice, short and chubby, and when I was a child
she worked at the Savoy Hotel, both in the laundry and as a
chambermaid. She was a very hard worker, and I don't think
she minded it. She even met a few film stars and celebrities!*

*She was engaged to a man but broke it off. Then she went up
north for a while, and we discovered later that she had a baby,
which was sent to Australia. This must have been in about 1962.*

The man she was engaged to was found dead almost fifteen years later: he was a drinker, a down-and-out, and he must have kept something with her name and address on it, because the police called and she had to go and identify his body.

By that time, she had married and had two children. She's lived on the Haygate Estate in Elephant and Castle for thirty years – and now they're going to knock it down and she's going to be rehoused. She's not happy about that. She's very religious, and recently, because she can't get out much, the priest has been coming round to the house to give her communion. She loves the soaps, especially Coronation Street, *and she's very proud of her collection of Waterford glass and Royal Albert china.*

Auntie Kay, my godmother, was older than my dad and came over to London before him. She worked as a domestic in the old Belgrave Children's Hospital at the Oval. The jobs were advertised in the Irish press and paid less than the ones you procured yourself. She lived on Camberwell Green in a Victorian tenement building that's since been demolished. She's dead now. Both Mary and Kay had very dark hair and complexions. They reminded me of Romanies.

Two other sisters stayed in Ireland. There's Aunt Teresa, who lives in Dublin. I don't see her often. Aunt Philly still lives in Limerick, in the same terrace house they were all born in, though it's much improved now. She used to come over to London to see us when I was young, and Dad would take her out sightseeing and shopping. She was rather glamorous and reminded me of a film star. She worked in an office and got married to someone with a good job in the building industry, and they had one daughter. They're quite well off.

I married a Muslim and later got divorced. Although they're very keen Catholics, my aunts didn't seem to mind or think my choices were odd, and they loved it when I went into nursing. And now they're particularly fond of my elder son Gabriel, who's very chatty and sociable. He's training to be a psychiatric nurse.

Then there were the aunties. It's always struck me as odd that we never called the men they were married to 'Uncle', probably because it was a word used to refer to the pawn shop. Anyway, the aunties were our neighbours in an old-fashioned council block in Kennington which had a courtyard and balconies running along each floor. This meant that everyone could look out for everyone else. I can remember a horse-drawn milk cart delivering every day.

On the ground floor was Auntie Midge. Her husband was Italian, and she cooked things that seemed very exotic to us, like ravioli – not out of a tin. She was found dead in bed when I was nine. That was really my first encounter with death.

Next to us was Auntie Vowles, who lived with her mother. I used to run their errands for them, as a way of earning pocket money. I went down Lambeth Walk to the butcher's to buy them breast of lamb – they were always making stews with pearl barley. I bought them their cigarettes too – it was legal in those days. Their flat smelt of mothballs, it was very clean and tidy, and I remember it had a picture of a baby in a cradle called A Little Bit of Heaven. *One day they gave us their old wooden bed, with a nice soft mattress. I slept in it, but the first morning I woke up I was covered in blisters. My dad thought they were bedbugs and got rid of the mattress – but in fact, I had chickenpox.*

On the other side was Auntie Joan, who held a Sunday school in her front room and took my mum to hear Billy

Graham. She had two daughters of her own and used to foster black children. They weren't allowed television, and when Churchill died, they came into our house to watch the funeral.

Further along there was Auntie Peggy, who was married to a coalman, and directly above us Auntie Lil, known as Bingo Lil for obvious reasons. Auntie Toni was married to a long-distance lorry driver, and they had a flat on two storeys. She was petite and always dressed just so, in the fashions of the day. I loved the fur rug they had in their sitting room, the sort that you could dig your feet into.

Nobody ever locked their doors; everybody would hang over the balconies chatting. I can only ever remember one crime, when a boy broke in and stole the sixpences from our gas meter. But then there was nothing to steal: we didn't have a fridge or a washing machine or a phone.

The aunties would come in for a cup of tea, but never for a meal. And apart from a glass of sherry at Christmas, drink was something you went to the pub for. Everybody smoked, everybody shared. Scandals? Well, one girl got pregnant and was sent away to a mother-and-baby home. There was quite a lot of what would nowadays be called domestic violence, though I never saw anything really nasty.

Everyone got on very well, with the women being the hub of the community. I can't remember that my mum ever had a friend outside the block – her only friends were the neighbour aunties. There were two black ladies living there too. We got on fine with them, but we never called them auntie.

The flats were demolished in 1971, and we were all moved to new buildings elsewhere in the neighbourhood. In the new blocks, the flats were closed in. They didn't have the old court-yard and balconies, and that was a great mistake. In fact, I think that's where it all began to go wrong, because it destroyed the sense of community.

Where have all the aunties gone? I've no idea, we lost track. My mum's dead, and I imagine many of them have died too.

My children never called anyone aunt or auntie – I don't know if that's my fault, but it seems to be a habit that is dying out everywhere now, except among Africans and West Indians.

Lou Woodvine

My mum was one of ten, so I had four blood aunts and five uncles. All of them were married, and my uncles' wives were my aunts too.

I can't remember much about them, because when they got married, they moved away. Aunt Alice was in service; she was

married to Uncle George. Aunt Annie was married to Uncle
Joe, and they lived on a farm in Ashford, Middlesex, and had a
horse and cart with which they used to take stuff down to the
greengrocer's. Aunt Rose married Uncle Jim; she didn't do a lot
because she had nine children.

When the men were away, my aunts all used to get together
with my mum for fun and games in a pub round here, and
when Mum knew that Dad was coming home on leave from the
navy, she'd shout, 'That's it, girls, time to clean up.'

I'm an aunt, but so many times over I've lost count. I haven't
met all my nieces and nephews, and I certainly wouldn't recognize them. When I see any of them, I have to ask them who their
parents are. I'm not close to any of them.

Joyce Bevington

I'm eighty-eight, but I have two aunts who are still alive. One
lives up north somewhere, I don't know where. The other one
lives in Slough, and we keep in touch by phone. There was
hardly any age difference between us, so we were more like sisters. She's called Peggy, but I never called her 'Aunt', never. She
had a good life. Being the youngest of six, her mother liked her
and encouraged her, and when she got married, she encouraged
her children too. Peggy worked at Hoover's and then in a gar-
ment factory. She married one of her cousins – but not a first
cousin – when he came out of the army. Peggy is very outgoing.
Her great hobby is typing letters. She's not a strict churchgoer
herself, but she wouldn't interfere with anyone who wanted to
go. She's religious in her own way – in fact, she does everything
in her own way.

My life was rough when I was a kid. My mother didn't really want me, and I was put somewhere in Surrey when I was a baby, then I was pushed around all over the place. I never knew who my father was. I know I've got a half-brother, but I've never seen him and I don't know what his name is – he lives in Wiltshire, in a village called something like Hull.

My mother and I were never close. 'You and I tolerate each other,' she said to me at the end – she died when she was ninety-three. There was no love between us, but I looked after her for the last three years of her life. Really and truly, I'd have been better off on my own from the beginning. There was nothing there. I was always much happier with Peggy.

Nell Donoghue

I had a very sweet aunt called Aunt Vic. She was my mother's sister, and when I was little, she used to live in our house, because there was no money around in those days. Then she and her husband moved to Dagenham in Essex, after the council built all these houses. My sister and I used to go down there every summer for six weeks for a holiday – this was before the war. It was marvellous, we had the time of our lives. They had an old piano in their front parlour, and they'd take us to Southend and to the pictures. There was this garden party too every year, and because Vic was such a great dressmaker, my sister and I won second prize, all dressed up in black velvet as the little princes in the tower. We always came home with a new dress Vic had run up for us on her sewing machine. She didn't have any children of her own. That's what it was, I suppose.

11

Aunties

Most of the aunts in this book are blood-related sisters of a parent, and it would be fair to generalize that they are the source of the most intense love that courses to or from a niece or nephew; a spousal aunt, to whom one is related only by an uncle's marriage, rarely provokes such emotion.

But there is another sort of aunt to consider too, one with no place on the family tree: this is the auntie, in the sense specified by the *Oxford English Dictionary* as 'a term of familiarity or respect applied to an elderly woman', almost synonymous with the Tudor English 'Goody' (short for 'goodwife') and applicable to just about any post-menopausal female who might otherwise be call 'ducky', 'dear' or 'love'. In Britain, it has historically been a word and a concept more prevalent among the working class; the middle class has tended to be more particular about distinguishing an honorary auntie from a blood-related aunt, while the upper middle class generally eschews it altogether. It can also substitute for other familial titles; when I was a small child, the old lady everybody called Auntie Jo was, in fact, my great-grandmother – something that was never explained to me and which left me very confused.

The *OED* qualifies its definition of auntie as something 'applied esp. to a Negress'. It has certainly long been a very popular expression in Afro-American culture. In *Uncle Tom's Cabin* (1852), for example, Uncle Tom's wife is called Aunt

Chloe; she is, as Harriet Beecher Stowe puts it, 'aunt to nobody in particular, but [an aunt] to human nature generally'. (See also the discussion of Aunt Jemima's Pancake Mix on p. 195–6.)

The great majority of aunties are passing figures in the parade of life, so called only as a sort of courtesy title of no real emotional or even practical significance beyond the aura of benevolence they attract and emanate. 'These aunties,' wrote Penney Hames in a recent article in the *Daily Telegraph*, 'were the sort you saw daily. The sort who lived only a hopscotch away, swapped Rice Krispie biscuit recipes with your mum, knew that you did swimming on a Wednesday and stayed downstairs with a brandy and *The Generation Game* when your parents went out for the evening.'

But aunties can be more than good neighbours by another name: they can also take on the responsibilities that come with the role of a blood aunt – surrogate aunts, one could call them. Typical of these was the novelist Winifred Holtby, who enjoyed an intense friendship and working partnership with the pacifist and feminist Vera Brittain that dated back to their Oxford days. When Vera was swept up by the success of her First World War memoir *Testament of Youth* in the mid-1930s, it was Winifred who stepped in to look after her young children. Winifred, unmarried and childless herself, developed a relationship with little John and Shirley (later famous as the politician Shirley Williams) that was warmer and closer than the one they enjoyed with their formidable mother. 'When Winifred was in charge,' Shirley recalled forty years later, 'my brother and I would pile up tons of cushions, and sit on top pretending to be maharajahs, or dress up in old bonnets and bowlers as fashionable Victorians.' Winifred died tragically young, when Shirley was barely five, but her memory remained vivid.

Such aunties can have a profound influence on a child, perhaps because they stand at one remove from the family and its norms. Wallace Shawn's haunting play *Aunt Dan and Lemon* (1985) records this phenomenon in the case of a sensitive eleven-year-old girl known as Lemon (actually Leonora), who is in thrall to her parents' best friend, known as Aunt Dan. Aunt Dan is not conventionally benign. She is sexually omnivorous and a product of the liberations of the 1960s who has ended up far to the right politically, with an obsessional crush on Henry Kissinger. 'There's something inside us that likes to kill,' she insists.

Lemon's parents drop Dan, finding her politics too hot to handle, but Lemon is hypnotized by this weirdly charismatic woman and continues to see her well into her teens. At one point there is a frisson between them that suggests they might go to bed together, but it passes, and Aunt Dan dies when Lemon is nineteen. Lemon is left disturbed by Dan, with a respect for Nazism that she can't quite explain. At the end of the play, Lemon addresses the audience:

> Because if there's one thing I learned from Aunt Dan, I suppose you could say it was a kind of honesty. It's easy to say we should all be loving and sweet, but meanwhile we're enjoying a certain way of life – we're actually living – due to the existence of certain other people who are willing to take the job of killing on their own backs, and it's not a bad thing every once in a while to admit that that's the way we're living, and even to give to those certain people a tiny, fractional crumb of thanks.

An auntie can also be a foster parent: the great actor of the early nineteenth century Edmund Kean was brought up by Charlotte Tidswell, a two-bit actress he called Aunt Tid, who had been mistress to both his uncle and the Duke of Norfolk (Kean put it about that he was the bastard son of the latter, but this was untrue). Why did Aunt Tid endure him? As a child, he was so obstreperous and runaway that she had to tie a dog collar round his neck with the inscription 'Bring this boy to Miss Tidswell, 12 Tavistock Row.' Was she compelled by some first intimation of his histrionic genius? Certainly he later paid tribute to her as the primary inspiration of his theatrical career and their relationship would survive even Kean's self-destructive superstar capacity to fall out with anyone who had helped, admired or loved him. He acted at her final benefit performance in 1822, and ten years later she was there to nurse him in his pathetically washed-up dying days.

This was a relatively happy ending. Rudyard Kipling's autobiography *Something of Myself* tells another story. When he was seven, his itinerant parents parked him (while they were stationed in India) in what he describes as a 'house of desolation' in Southsea. It was owned by a Mrs Sarah Holloway, who had to be called 'Aunty'. A domestic tyrant, as well as a member of the austere Plymouth Brethren sect, her sadistic bullying and torturing went way beyond anything experienced by his contemporary Hector Munro, similarly dumped in Devon (see p. 164–5). Kipling's bitterness at her treatment 'drained' him, he thought, 'of any capacity for real, personal hate for the rest of my days'.

The auntie is a particularly potent figure in India, crossing several linguistic and cultural domains. Probal Dasgupta's study *India's Auntie Tongue* (1993) explores auntie as 'a significant fact in the domain of Indian English usage', quoting Kamal K. Sridhar's view that she 'functions as a marker of Westernised sophistication among the upwardly mobile middle classes in urban and semi-urban India'. In Indian English, it emerges, 'middle and upper-middle class children who go to English-medium schools address their friends' mothers as Auntie'. This cannot be new: in *The Raj Quartet*, Paul Scott's novels about the British withdrawal from India in the 1940s, the ingenuous Daphne Manners shyly asks whether she can call Lady Chatterjee 'Auntie'. Interestingly, 'auntie' is also a common Indian slang term for a prostitute or a madam. The *OED* doesn't record this usage after the seventeenth century, but it may have continued to have some oral currency in Britain – in Montagu Slater's libretto for Benjamin Britten's opera *Peter Grimes* (1945), set in Suffolk in the early nineteenth century, a woman known universally as Auntie runs a pub that doubles as a bawdy house, populated by her 'nieces'.*

'Auntie' has many other euphemistic applications, all redolent of cosy comfort and moral rectitude. In the US, Auntie is the name of an anti-litter campaign and a firm selling politically progressive T-shirts bearing anti-Bush slogans. In New Zealand, The Aunties are the nation's 'most innovative and

---

* Only two blood aunts feature in the operatic repertory. One is the monstrous Zia Principessa, 'Aunt Princess', in Puccini's *Suor Angelica*. The other is Brünnhilde in Wagner's *Der Ring des Nibelungen*. She really belongs in the chapter on X-Rated Aunts, as she is technically the lover of her nephew Siegfried, via her father Wotan, who is also father to Siegfried's parents, the twins Siegmund and Sieglinde. The incestuous nature of the latter's union is a bone of contention in the *Ring*'s second instalment *Die Walküre*, but Wagner doesn't pursue it when it comes to Siegfried and Brünnhilde getting together in *Siegfried*.

loved family entertainers'; at Aston University, 'Aunties' is the name of a scheme in which senior students befriend bewildered freshers. The British Broadcasting Corporation was for many years nicknamed Auntie, or Auntie Beeb. Nobody can trace the coiner of this jibe, but according to Asa Briggs's authoritative *History of Broadcasting in the United Kingdom*, it seems to date from the post-war years, when the BBC established a strict code of taste and decency which sought to lead the nation's ethical standards by example (perhaps not such a bad idea, one might think, in the era of *Big Brother* and worse). This wasn't just a matter of censoring steamy love scenes: it also involved a ban on the display of betting odds at the races and the satirical impersonation of politicians. The force of the joke weakened in the 1960s, when programmes such as *Till Death Us Do Part*, *Z Cars* and *That Was the Week that Was* broke the taboos, and the mantle of Auntie passed to Mary Whitehouse. Nowadays the press tends to wheel the epithet out only when a commentator wishes to mock the BBC's 'commitment to public service broadcasting'.

The most familiar manifestation of the auntie, however, is the Agony Aunt. The practice of writing to 'a lady' to seek advice on romantic quandaries goes back to the mid-eighteenth century, when a middle-aged ex-actress called Mrs Eliza Haywood solicited letters from the public in a short-lived journal called *The Female Spectator*. Her aim was 'to check the enormous growth in luxury, to reform the morals and improve the manners of an Age, by all confess'd degenerate and sunk'.

Robin Scott's interesting history of this journalistic phenomenon can't locate the point at which such columnists became known as 'agony aunts', but she notes that the hero of P. G. Wodehouse's novel *Sam the Sudden*, published in 1925, takes a job as Aunt Isobel in *Pyke's Home Journal*, continuing the noble Victorian tradition of heterosexual moustachioed men posing as pseudonymous Agony Aunts. But by the 1950s, the Agony Aunt had become openly female, and the advice of the likes of Evelyn Home, Mary Grant, Claire Rayner and Marjorie Proops was sought on the brave new world of sexual technique, open relationships and chemical contraception. An interesting oddity is someone on the internet who calls herself Auntie Kate who answers questions sent to her via a website called CousinCouples.com dealing exclusively with the delicate problems faced by cousins who have become romantically involved with each other.

In Europe and the US, the domestic use of the 'Auntie' honorific is now on the decline (except, perhaps, among pious Afro-Caribbeans). This can largely be ascribed to changes in social etiquette, which means that it is no longer impolite for a youngster to call an adult woman by her unadorned Christian name, 'Auntie' seeming somewhat quaint, if not vaguely offensive, in its implication of prim propriety and middle age. In her *Daily Telegraph* article, Penney Hames concluded that 'from a 21st-century perspective, there's something about "auntie" that reeks of an outdated and almost embarrassing preciousness and deference. As a child, I loved it, but as an adult, I squirm. Its passing is a sign of the times, much like wall-mounted tea caddies, Formica tabletops and Green Shield Stamps. We love their memory, but we don't want them back.'

*

Auntliness is most often associated with comfort – even an agony aunt assuages the pain. Aunt Vicki, an interesting exception to the rule, lives near Fort Worth airport in Texas. Her website informs us that she is 'an experienced, strict but understanding, stern but loving disciplinarian'. A photograph of a plain, plump, middle-aged woman in glasses with a slightly exasperated expression does indeed seem to embody these qualities – she could be a librarian or a primary-school teacher. But the sort of comfort this aunt offers is exquisitely and deliberately painful: for in her hand she clutches a wooden implement the size of a ping-pong bat, and the caption reads, 'You – get over here – NOW!'

For Aunt Vicki 'loves to spank', and she is 'very good at it' too. 'I use the over-the-knee position as well as a spanking stool . . . There's nothing more satisfying than the feel of my hairbrush or paddle smacking a naughty bare bottom,' she continues. Together with Aunt Prissy – her sister, it is claimed, though the photograph suggests a male transvestite – she runs a service designed to satisfy a common sexual fantasy, whose most celebrated modern exegete was the critic Kenneth Tynan.

'I have been a strict disciplinarian most of my life, beginning with helping to raise my brothers and sisters, and then raising my own children,' she says. 'And now I have continued to administer discipline when needed, in the form of corporal punishment, combined with scolding, corner time, humiliation, panty training and more.' Using hairbrushes, straps, belts, canes, crops, rulers and wooden spoons, she administers 'spanking, paddling, caning, whipping, strapping, switching and any other method that seems effective . . . When you have a spanking session with me you will certainly feel you have been punished.'

Aunt Vicki is not, she insists, 'a leather dominatrix', and what she provides is 'domestic-style discipline . . . I am not sadistic, but I am firm and will spank as hard as the situation calls for.' The premises of her 'spanking house' contain a schoolroom and a sheriff's office, and she has 'plans to build an authentic woodshed out the back so that I really can take some of you "out to the woodshed". If anyone wants to help with labor and/or materials, then contact me.'

Aunt Vicki's gifts find her besieged. Those who crave a domestic-style whacking must fill in a questionnaire and send her a $50 deposit, but she warns that it may be months before she can deal with you. Meanwhile, people write in and chat. A thirty-two-year-old woman from Florida, for example: 'I have a very young sweet face and a soft white backside. Generally, I'm very loving and generous, but sometimes I get too self-centered. Last naughty thing I did . . . I forgot to pay all my bills on time. How would you handle a girl like me?' Aunt Vicki responds by offering the prospect of a good purgative thrashing with a hairbrush.

Mom Vicki, Grandma Vicki, Sister Vicki – how would their spanking appeal differ?

FLORA JOLL ON CLAUDE

*Some people call her Candia, but to me she's always been
Claude. She's actually my godmother, but I've always thought
of her as my aunt. My mother and she were at boarding school
together, and apparently Claude turned up on the first day in
an inappropriate school uniform and everybody thought she
must be rather more exotic than they were used to, but my
mother thought she looked glamorous and fun. They became
very close friends, and because there were difficulties in her own
home, she came to my grandparents' house in the Outer
Hebrides during the holidays. Essentially, they ended up adopting her and my grandfather gave her away at her wedding.*

*I ended up being particularly close to her because I was
unhappy at boarding school in Oxford, and because Claude
lived there, I ended up lodging in her house for long periods. I
still don't think I could survive without seeing her – I need to be
able to sit in her kitchen and talk about books and hear her
advice on my typically teenage life.*

*I'd love to be as hospitable as she is. There are always teeter-
ing piles of books everywhere and a constant supply of food and
drink. She's a writer and needs time alone, but she has never
not answered the doorbell and offered at least five cups of tea.
I'd love to have that kind of a beautiful house, people trooping
in and chatting for hours and children of all ages everywhere.*

*I appreciate Claude as a listener all the more because in my
house you have to scream to be heard. There are five of us, and
we're all very, very loud and quite confident. You just have to
jump into conversations whenever you get the chance. And now
I'm at Cambridge, I feel I've never met people with more taste*

for self-analysis – they can talk about themselves till the cows come home.

But with Claude, I have real conversation – about my family and the latest boyfriends, about her life and all the people in it, and all the time I know that her mind is so rich that there are about twenty-five things going on inside it as she's talking to me. Books are a very big part of it all: the family mantra is never to go anywhere without a book in your pocket, and ever since she told me about Tintin when we were on a boat in the Hebrides, Claude and I have been talking about them. I went to the Edinburgh Book Festival with her last summer and heard her read her own poetry. I'd never heard it before, and the experience was awe-inspiring – I couldn't get over how vulnerable she was prepared to make herself in a public place. Afterwards she said, 'Come and have lunch with Julian,' and of course it was Julian Barnes. I spilled Caesar salad in his lap and he was very nice about it.

I don't know if I'm going to write too. I'm not sure I have anything original to say, but I suppose I'd like to have a go. I tend to write only when something doesn't make sense and I try to clear my mind by putting it down on paper. Claude won the Vogue *Talent Competition when she was 15. I thought I'd go in for it too, with a short story about modelling. In the end I missed the deadline, but I gave it to Claude to read. I was worried when I showed her what I'd done, because I knew she wouldn't lie or pretend that she thought it was good. But she said, 'There's something in your writing,' and that meant a lot to me.*

My mother is eminently sensible, but I think any other mother might feel funny about our relationship. But Claude and

Mum are so close, they understand each other better than anyone else in the world. Claude's own three children are the same sort of ages as me and my siblings, but circumstances have kept us apart a bit.

I have lots of real aunts too. Four on my mother's side. They're all ardent feminists and about three feet shorter than I am – very loving and dynamos of energy. On my father's side there are three. And so hundreds of cousins all over the place. There's one aunt in Italy and one in Australia, and sometimes they meet up and all look exactly the same. You can rely on them to tell us when we're out of line and to give us vital information about our parents that they are too embarrassed to own up to. And of course, they all know Claude, so there are stories about her too. For instance, I was interested to hear how she used to wear high heels to make herself look even taller. Like me she's a six-footer, but I'd never do that – I hunch.

MARY POSTGATE
by Rudyard Kipling

Of Miss Mary Postgate, Lady McCausland wrote that she was 'thoroughly conscientious, tidy, companionable, and ladylike. I am very sorry to part with her, and shall always be interested in her welfare.'

Miss Fowler engaged her on this recommendation, and to her surprise, for she had had experience of companions, found that it was true. Miss Fowler was nearer sixty than fifty at the time, but though she needed care she did not exhaust her attendant's vitality. On the contrary, she gave out, stimu-

latingly and with reminiscences. Her father had been a minor
Court official in the days when the Great Exhibition of 1851
had just set its seal on Civilisation made perfect. Some of Miss
Fowler's tales, none the less, were not always for the young.
Mary was not young, and though her speech was as colourless
as her eyes or her hair, she was never shocked. She listened
unflinchingly to every one; said at the end, 'How interesting!'
or 'How shocking!' as the case might be, and never again
referred to it, for she prided herself on a trained mind, which
'did not dwell on these things.' She was, too, a treasure at
domestic accounts, for which the village tradesmen, with their
weekly books, loved her not. Otherwise she had no enemies;
provoked no jealousy even among the plainest; neither gossip
nor slander had ever been traced to her; she supplied the odd
place at the Rector's or the Doctor's table at half an hour's
notice; she was a sort of public aunt to very many small children of the village street, whose parents, while accepting
everything, would have been swift to resent what they called
'patronage'; she served on the Village Nursing Committee as
Miss Fowler's nominee when Miss Fowler was crippled by
rheumatoid arthritis, and came out of six months' fortnightly
meetings equally respected by all the cliques.

And when Fate threw Miss Fowler's nephew, an unlovely
orphan of eleven, on Miss Fowler's hands, Mary Postgate
stood to her share of the business of education as practised in
private and public schools. She checked printed clothes-lists,
and unitemised bills of extras; wrote to Head and House masters, matrons, nurses and doctors, and grieved or rejoiced
over half-term reports. Young Wyndham Fowler repaid her in
his holidays by calling her 'Gatepost,' 'Postey,' or 'Packthread,'

by thumping her between her narrow shoulders or by chasing
her bleating, round the garden, her large mouth open, her
large nose high in the air, at a stiff-necked shamble very like a
camel's. Later on he filled the house with clamour, argument,
and harangues as to his personal needs, likes and dislikes, and
the limitations of 'you women,' reducing Mary to tears of
physical fatigue, or, when he chose to be humorous, of helpless laughter. At crises, which multiplied as he grew older, she
was his ambassadress and his interpretress to Miss Fowler,
who had no large sympathy with the young; a vote in his
interest at the councils on his future; his sewing-woman,
strictly accountable for mislaid boots and garments; always
his butt and his slave.

And when he decided to become a solicitor, and had
entered an office in London; when his greeting had changed
from 'Hullo, Postey, you old beast,' to 'Mornin, Packthread,'
there came a war which, unlike all wars that Mary could
remember, did not stay decently outside England and in the
newspapers, but intruded on the lives of people whom she
knew. As she said to Miss Fowler, it was 'most vexatious.' It
took the Rector's son who was going into business with his
elder brother; it took the Colonel's nephew on the eve of fruit-
farming in Canada; it took Mrs. Grant's son who, his mother
said, was devoted to the ministry; and, very early indeed, it
took Wynn Fowler, who announced on a postcard that he had
joined the Flying Corps and wanted a cardigan waistcoat.

'He must go, and he must have the waistcoat,' said Miss
Fowler. So Mary got the proper-sized needles and wool, while
Miss Fowler told the men of her establishment – two garden-
ers and an odd man, aged sixty – that those who could join

the Army had better do so. The gardeners left. Cheape, the odd man, stayed on, and was promoted to the gardener's cottage. The cook, scorning to be limited in luxuries, also left, after a spirited scene with Miss Fowler, and took the housemaid with her. Miss Fowler gazetted Nellie, Cheape's seventeen-year-old daughter, to the vacant post; Mrs. Cheape to the rank of cook with occasional cleaning bouts; and the reduced establishment moved forward smoothly.

Wynn demanded an increase in his allowance. Miss Fowler, who always looked facts in the face, said, 'He must have it. The chances are he won't live long to draw it, and if three hundred makes him happy – –'

Wynn was grateful, and came over, in his tight-buttoned uniform, to say so. His training centre was not thirty miles away, and his talk was so technical that it had to be explained by charts of the various types of machines. He gave Mary such a chart.

'And you'd better study it, Postey,' he said. 'You'll be seeing a lot of 'em soon.' So Mary studied the chart, but when Wynn next arrived to swell and exalt himself before his womenfolk, she failed badly in cross-examination, and he rated her as in the old days.

'You look more or less like a human being,' he said in his new Service voice. 'You must have had a brain at some time in your past. What have you done with it? Where'd you keep it? A sheep would know more than you do, Postey. You're lamentable. You are less use than an empty tin can, you dowey old cassowary.'

'I suppose that's how your superior officer talks to you?' said Miss Fowler from her chair.

'But Postey doesn't mind,' Wynn replied. 'Do you, Pack-thread?'

'Why? Was Wynn saying anything? I shall get this right next time you come,' she muttered, and knitted her pale brows again over the diagrams of Taubes, Farmans, and Zeppelins.

In a few weeks the mere land and sea battles which she read to Miss Fowler after breakfast passed her like idle breath. Her heart and her interest were high in the air with Wynn, who had finished 'rolling' (whatever that might be) and gone on from a 'taxi' to a machine more or less his own. One morning it circled over their very chimneys, alighted on Vegg's Heath, almost outside the garden gate, and Wynn came in, blue with cold, shouting for food. He and she drew Miss Fowler's bath-chair, as they had often done, along the Heath foot-path to look at the biplane. Mary observed that 'it smelt very badly.'

'Postey, I believe you think with your nose,' said Wynn. 'I know you don't with your mind. Now, what type's that?'

'I'll go and get the chart,' said Mary.

'You're hopeless! You haven't the mental capacity of a white mouse,' he cried, and explained the dials and the sockets for bomb-dropping till it was time to mount and ride the wet clouds once more.

'Ah!' said Mary, as the stinking thing flared upward. 'Wait till our Flying Corps gets to work! Wynn says it's much safer than in the trenches.'

'I wonder,' said Miss Fowler. 'Tell Cheape to come and tow me home again.'

'It's all downhill. I can do it,' said Mary, 'if you put the brake on.' She laid her lean self against the pushing-bar and home they trundled.

'Now, be careful you aren't heated and catch a chill,' said overdressed Miss Fowler.

'Nothing makes me perspire,' said Mary. As she bumped the chair under the porch she straightened her long back. The exertion had given her a colour, and the wind had loosened a wisp of hair across her forehead. Miss Fowler glanced at her.

'What do you ever think of, Mary?' she demanded suddenly.

'Oh, Wynn says he wants another three pairs of stockings – as thick as we can make them.'

'Yes. But I mean the things that women think about. Here you are, more than forty – –'

'Forty-four,' said truthful Mary.

'Well?'

'Well?' Mary offered Miss Fowler her shoulder as usual.

'And you've been with me ten years now.'

'Let's see,' said Mary. 'Wynn was eleven when he came. He's twenty now, and I came two years before that. It must be eleven.'

'Eleven! And you've never told me anything that matters in all that while. Looking back, it seems to me that I've done all the talking.'

'I'm afraid I'm not much of a conversationalist. As Wynn says, I haven't the mind. Let me take your hat.'

Miss Fowler, moving stiffly from the hip, stamped her rubber-tipped stick on the tiled hall floor. 'Mary, aren't you anything except a companion? Would you ever have been anything except a companion?'

Mary hung up the garden hat on its proper peg. 'No,' she said after consideration. 'I don't imagine I ever should.

But I've no imagination, I'm afraid.'

She fetched Miss Fowler her eleven-o'clock glass of Con-trexéville.

That was the wet December when it rained six inches to the month, and the women went abroad as little as might be. Wynn's flying chariot visited them several times, and for two mornings (he had warned her by postcard) Mary heard the thresh of his propellers at dawn. The second time she ran to the window, and stared at the whitening sky. A little blur passed overhead. She lifted her lean arms towards it.

That evening at six o'clock there came an announcement in an official envelope that Second Lieutenant W. Fowler had been killed during a trial flight. Death was instantaneous. She read it and carried it to Miss Fowler.

'I never expected anything else,' said Miss Fowler; 'but I'm sorry it happened before he had done anything.'

The room was whirling round Mary Postgate, but she found herself quite steady in the midst of it.

'Yes,' she said. 'It's a great pity he didn't die in action after he had killed somebody.'

'He was killed instantly. That's one comfort,' Miss Fowler went on.

'But Wynn says the shock of a fall kills a man at once – whatever happens to the tanks,' quoted Mary.

The room was coming to rest now. She heard Miss Fowler say impatiently, 'But why can't we cry, Mary?' and herself replying, 'There's nothing to cry for. He has done his duty as much as Mrs. Grant's son did.'

'And when he died, she came and cried all the morning,' said Miss Fowler. 'This only makes me feel tired – terribly tired. Will you help me to bed, please, Mary? – And I think I'd like the hot-water bottle.'

So Mary helped her and sat beside, talking of Wynn in his riotous youth.

'I believe,' said Miss Fowler suddenly, 'that old people and young people slip from under a stroke like this. The middle-aged feel it most.'

'I expect that's true,' said Mary, rising. 'I'm going to put away the things in his room now. Shall we wear mourning?'

'Certainly not,' said Miss Fowler. 'Except, of course, at the funeral. I can't go. You will. I want you to arrange about his being buried here. What a blessing it didn't happen at Salisbury!'

Every one, from the Authorities of the Flying Corps to the Rector, was most kind and sympathetic. Mary found herself for the moment in a world where bodies were in the habit of being despatched by all sorts of conveyances to all sorts of places. And at the funeral two young men in buttoned-up uniforms stood beside the grave and spoke to her afterwards.

'You're Miss Postgate, aren't you?' said one, 'Fowler told me about you. He was a good chap – a first-class fellow – a great loss.'

'Great loss!' growled his companion. 'We're all awfully sorry.'

'How high did he fall from?' Mary whispered.

'Pretty nearly four thousand feet, I should think, didn't he? You were up that day, Monkey?'

'All of that,' the other child replied. 'My bar made three thousand, and I wasn't as high as him by a lot.'

'Then that's all right,' said Mary. 'Thank you very much.'

They moved away as Mrs. Grant flung herself weeping on Mary's flat chest, under the lych-gate, and cried, 'I know how it feels! I know how it feels!'

'But both his parents are dead,' Mary returned, as she fended her off. 'Perhaps they've all met by now,' she added vaguely as she escaped towards the coach.

'I've thought of that too,' wailed Mrs. Grant; 'but then he'll be practically a stranger to them. Quite embarrassing!'

Mary faithfully reported every detail of the ceremony to Miss Fowler, who, when she described Mrs. Grant's outburst, laughed aloud.

'Oh, how Wynn would have enjoyed it! He was always utterly unreliable at funerals. D'you remember – –' And they talked of him again, each piecing out the other's gaps. 'And now,' said Miss Fowler, 'we'll pull up the blinds and we'll have a general tidy. That always does us good. Have you seen to Wynn's things?'

'Everything – since he first came,' said Mary. 'He was never destructive – even with his toys.'

They faced that neat room.

'It can't be natural not to cry,' Mary said at last. 'I'm so afraid you'll have a reaction.'

'As I told you, we old people slip from under the stroke. It's you I'm afraid for. Have you cried yet?'

'I can't. It only makes me angry with the Germans.'

'That's sheer waste of vitality,' said Miss Fowler. 'We must live till the war's finished.' She opened a full wardrobe. 'Now, I've been thinking things over. This is my plan. All his civilian clothes can be given away – Belgian refugees, and so on.'

Mary nodded. 'Boots, collars, and gloves?'

'They came back yesterday with his Flying Corps clothes' – Mary pointed to a roll on the little iron bed.

'Ah, but keep his Service things. Some one may be glad of them later. Do you remember his sizes?'

'Five feet eight and a half; thirty-six inches round the chest. But he told me he's just put on an inch and a half. Ill mark it on a label and tie it on his sleeping-bag.'

'So that disposes of that,' said Miss Fowler, tapping the palm of one hand with the ringed third finger of the other. 'What a waste it all is! We'll get his old school trunk tomorrow and pack his civilian clothes.'

'And the rest?' said Mary. 'His books and pictures and the games and the toys – and – and the rest?'

'My plan is to burn every single thing,' said Miss Fowler. 'Then we shall know where they are and no one can handle them afterwards. What do you think?'

'I think that would be much the best,' said Mary. 'But there's such a lot of them.'

'We'll burn them in the destructor,' said Miss Fowler.

This was an open-air furnace for the consumption of refuse; a little circular four-foot tower of pierced brick over an iron grating. Miss Fowler had noticed the design in a gardening journal years ago, and had had it built at the bottom of the garden. It suited her tidy soul, for it saved unsightly rubbish-heaps and the ashes lightened the stiff clay soil.

Mary considered for a moment, saw her way clear, and nodded again. They spent the evening putting away well-remembered civilian suits, underclothes that Mary had marked, and the regiments of very gaudy socks and ties. A second trunk was needed, and, after that, a little packing case,

and it was late next day when Cheape and the local carrier lifted them to the cart. The Rector luckily knew of a friend's son,
about five feet eight and a half inches high, to whom a complete Flying Corps outfit would be most acceptable, and sent
his gardener's son down with a barrow to take delivery of it.
The cap was hung up in Miss Fowler's bedroom, the belt in
Miss Postgate's; for, as Miss Fowler said, they had no desire to
make tea-party talk of them.

'That disposes of that,' said Miss Fowler. 'I'll leave the rest
to you, Mary. I can't run up and down the garden. You'd better take the big clothes-basket and get Nellie to help you.'

'I shall take the wheel-barrow and do it myself,' said Mary,
and for once in her life closed her mouth.

Miss Fowler, in moments of irritation, had called Mary
deadly methodical. She put on her oldest water-proof and
gardening-hat and her ever-slipping goloshes, for the weather
was on the edge of more rain. She gathered firelighters from
the kitchen, a half-scuttle of coals, and a faggot of brushwood.
These she wheeled in the barrow down the mossed paths to
the dank little laurel shrubbery where the destructor stood
under the drip of three oaks. She climbed the wire fence into
the Rector's glebe just behind, and from his tenant's rick
pulled two large armfuls of good hay, which she spread neatly
on the fire-bars. Next, journey by journey, passing Miss
Fowler's white face at the morning-room window each time,
she brought down in the towel-covered clothes-basket, on the
wheel-barrow, thumbed and used Hentys, Marryats, Levers,
Stevensons, Baroness Orczys, Garvices, schoolbooks, and
atlases, unrelated piles of the *Motor Cyclist*, the *Light Car*, and
catalogues of Olympia Exhibitions; the remnants of a fleet of

sailing-ships from nine-penny cutters to a three-guinea yacht; a prep-school dressing-gown; bats from three-and-sixpence to twenty-four shillings; cricket and tennis balls; disintegrated steam and clockwork locomotives with their twisted rails; a grey and red tin model of a submarine; a dumb gramophone and cracked records; golf-clubs that had to be broken across the knee, like his walking-sticks, and an assegai; photographs of private and public school cricket and football elevens, and his O.T.C. on the line of march; kodaks, and film-rolls; some pewters, and one real silver cup, for boxing competitions and Junior Hurdles; sheaves of school photographs; Miss Fowler's photograph; her own which he had borne off in fun and (good care she took not to ask!) had never returned; a playbox with a secret drawer; a load of flannels, belts, and jerseys, and a pair of spiked shoes unearthed in the attic; a packet of all the letters that Miss Fowler and she had ever written to him, kept for some absurd reason through all these years; a five-day attempt at a diary; framed pictures of racing motors in full Brooklands career, and load upon load of undistinguishable wreckage of tool-boxes, rabbit-hutches, electric batteries, tin soldiers, fret-saw outfits, and jig-saw puzzles.

Miss Fowler at the window watched her come and go, and said to herself, 'Mary's an old woman. I never realised it before.'

After lunch she recommended her to rest.

'I'm not in the least tired,' said Mary. 'I've got it all arranged. I'm going to the village at two o'clock for some paraffin. Nellie hasn't enough, and the walk will do me good.'

She made one last quest round the house before she start-ed, and found that she had overlooked nothing. It began to mist as soon as she had skirted Vegg's Heath, where Wynn used to descend – it seemed to her that she could almost hear the beat of his propellers overhead, but there was nothing to see. She hoisted her umbrella and lunged into the blind wet till she had reached the shelter of the empty village. As she came out of Mr. Kidd's shop with a bottle full of paraffin in her string shopping-bag, she met Nurse Eden, the village nurse, and fell into talk with her, as usual, about the village children. They were parting opposite the 'Royal Oak' when a gun, they fancied, was fired immediately behind the house. It was followed by a child's shriek dying into a wail.

'Accident!' said Nurse Eden promptly, and dashed through the empty bar, followed by Mary. They found Mrs. Gerritt, the publican's wife, who could only gasp and point to the yard, where a little cart-lodge was sliding sideways amid a clatter of tiles. Nurse Eden snatched up a sheet drying before the fire, ran out, lifted something from the ground, and flung the sheet round it. The sheet turned scarlet and half her uniform too, as she bore the load into the kitchen. It was little Edna Gerritt, aged nine, whom Mary had known since her perambulator days.

'Am I hurted bad?' Edna asked, and died between Nurse Eden's dripping hands. The sheet fell aside and for an instant, before she could shut her eyes, Mary saw the ripped and shredded body.

'It's a wonder she spoke at all,' said Nurse Eden. 'What in God's name was it?'

'A bomb,' said Mary.

'One o' the Zeppelins?'

'No. An aeroplane. I thought I heard it on the Heath but I

fancied it was one of ours. It must have shut off its engines as it came down. That's why we didn't notice it.'

'The filthy pigs!' said Nurse Eden, all white and shaken. 'See the pickle I'm in! Go and tell Dr. Hennis, Miss Postgate.' Nurse looked at the mother, who had dropped face down on the floor. 'She's only in a fit. Turn her over.'

Mary heaved Mrs. Gerrit right side up, and hurried off for the doctor. When she told her tale, he asked her to sit down in the surgery till he got her something.

'But I don't need it, I assure you,' said she. 'I don't think it would be wise to tell Miss Fowler about it, do you? Her heart is so irritable in this weather.'

Dr. Hennis looked at her admiringly as he packed up his bag.

'No. Don't tell anybody till we're sure,' he said, and hastened to the 'Royal Oak,' while Mary went on with the paraffin. The village behind her was as quiet as usual, for the news had not yet spread. She frowned a little to herself, the large nostrils expanded uglily, and from time to time she muttered a phrase which Wynn, who had never restrained himself before his women-folk, had applied to the enemy. 'Bloody pagans! They are bloody pagans. But,' she continued, falling back on the teaching that had made her what she was, 'one mustn't let one's mind dwell on these things.'

Before she reached the house Dr. Hennis, who was also a special constable, overtook her in his car.

'Oh, Miss Postgate,' he said, 'I wanted to tell you that that accident at the 'Royal Oak' was due to Gerritt's stable tumbling down. It's been dangerous for a long time. It ought to have been condemned.'

'I thought I heard an explosion too,' said Mary.

'You might have been misled by the beams snapping. I've been looking at 'em. They were dry-rotted through and through. Of course, as they broke, they would make a noise just like a gun.'

'Yes?' said Mary politely.

'Poor little Edna was playing underneath it,' he went on, still holding her with his eyes, 'and that and the tiles cut her to pieces, you see?'

'I saw it,' said Mary, shaking her head. 'I heard it too.'

'Well, we cannot be sure.' Dr. Hennis changed his tone completely. 'I know both you and Nurse Eden (I've been speaking to her) are perfectly trustworthy, and I can rely on you not to say anything – yet at least. It is no good to stir up people unless – –'

'Oh, I never do – anyhow,' said Mary, and Dr. Hennis went on to the country town.

After all, she told herself, it might, just possibly, have been the collapse of the old stable that had done all those things to poor little Edna. She was sorry she had even hinted at other things, but Nurse Eden was discretion itself. By the time she reached home the affair seemed increasingly remote by its very monstrosity. As she came in, Miss Fowler told her that a couple of aeroplanes had passed half an hour ago.

'I thought I heard them,' she replied, 'I'm going down to the garden now. I've got the paraffin.'

'Yes, but – what have you got on your boots? They're soaking wet. Change them at once.'

Not only did Mary obey, but she wrapped the boots in a newspaper, and put them into the string bag with the bottles.

So, armed with the longest kitchen poker, she left.

'It's raining again,' was Miss Fowler's last word, 'but – I know you won't be happy till that's disposed of.'

'It won't take long. I've got everything down there, and I've put the lid on the destructor to keep the wet out.'

The shrubbery was filling with twilight by the time she had completed her arrangements and sprinkled the sacrificial oil. As she lit the match that would burn her heart to ashes, she heard a groan or a grunt behind the dense Portugal laurels.

'Cheape?' she called impatiently, but Cheape, with his ancient lumbago, in his comfortable cottage would be the last man to profane the sanctuary. 'Sheep,' she concluded, and threw in the fusee. The pyre went up in a roar, and the immediate flame hastened night around her.

'How Wynn would have loved this!' she thought, stepping back from the blaze.

By its light she saw, half hidden behind a laurel not five paces away, a bare-headed man sitting very stiffly at the foot of one of the oaks. A broken branch lay across his lap – one booted leg protruding from beneath it. His head moved ceaselessly from side to side, but his body was as still as the tree's trunk. He was dressed – she moved sideways to look more closely – in a uniform something like Wynn's, with a flap buttoned across the chest. For an instant she had some idea that it might be one of the young flying men she had met at the funeral. But their heads were dark and glossy. This man's was as pale as a baby's, and so closely cropped that she could see the disgusting pink skin beneath. His lips moved.

'What do you say?' Mary moved towards him and stooped.

'Laty! Laty! Laty!' he muttered, while his hands picked at

the dead wet leaves. There was no doubt as to his nationality.
It made her so angry that she strode back to the destructor,
though it was still too hot to use the poker there. Wynn's
books seemed to be catching well. She looked up at the oak
behind the man; several of the light upper and two or three
rotten lower branches had broken and scattered their rubbish
on the shrubbery path. On the lowest fork a helmet with
dependent strings, showed like a bird's-nest in the light of a
long-tongued flame. Evidently this person had fallen through
the trees. Wynn had told her that it was quite possible for people to fall out of aeroplanes. Wynn told her, too, that trees
were useful things to break an aviator's fall, but in this case the
aviator must have been broken or he would have moved from
his queer position. He seemed helpless except for his horrible
rolling head. On the other hand, she could see a pistol case at
his belt – and Mary loathed pistols. Months ago, after reading
certain Belgian reports together, she and Miss Fowler had had
dealings with one – a huge revolver with flat-nosed bullets,
which latter, Wynn said, were forbidden by the rules of war to
be used against civilised enemies. 'They're good enough for
us,' Miss Fowler had replied. 'Show Mary how it works.' And
Wynn, laughing at the mere possibility of any such need, had
led the craven winking Mary into the Rector's disused quarry,
and had shown her how to fire the terrible machine. It lay
now in the top-left-hand drawer of her toilet-table – a memen-
to not included in the burning. Wynn would be pleased to see
how she was not afraid.

She slipped up to the house to get it. When she came
through the rain, the eyes in the head were alive with expectation. The mouth even tried to smile. But at sight of the

revolver its corners went down just like Edna Gerritt's. A tear
trickled from one eye, and the head rolled from shoulder to
shoulder as through trying to point out something.

'Cassée. Tout cassée,' it whimpered.

'What do you say?' said Mary disgustedly, keeping well to
one side, though only the head moved.

'Cassée,' it repeated. 'Che me rends. Le médicin! Toctor!'

'Nein!' said she, bringing all her small German to bear with
the big pistol. 'Ich haben der todt Kinder gesehn.'

The head was still. Mary's hand dropped. She had been
careful to keep her finger off the trigger for fear of accidents.
After a few moments' waiting, she returned to the destructor,
where the flames were falling, and churned up Wynn's char-
ring books with the poker. Again the head groaned for the
doctor.

'Stop that!' said Mary, and stamped her foot. 'Stop that, you
bloody pagan!'

The words came quite smoothly and naturally. They were
Wynn's own words, and Wynn was a gentleman who for no
consideration on earth would have torn little Edna into those
vividly coloured strips and strings. But this thing hunched
under the oak-tree had done that thing. It was no question of
reading horrors out of newspapers to Miss Fowler. Mary had
seen it with her own eyes on the 'Royal Oak' kitchen table.
She must not allow her mind to dwell upon it. Now Wynn was
dead, and everything connected with him was lumping and
rustling and tinkling under her busy poker into red black dust
and grey leaves of ash. The thing beneath the oak would die
too. Mary had seen death more than once. She came of a family that had a knack of dying under, as she told Miss Fowler,

'most distressing circumstances.' She would stay where she
was till she was entirely satisfied that It was dead – dead as
dear papa in the late 'eighties; aunt Mary in 'eighty-nine;
mamma in 'ninety-one; cousin Dick in 'ninety-five; Lady
McCausland's housemaid in 'ninety-nine; Lady McCausland's sister in nineteen hundred and one; Wynn buried five
days ago; and Edna Gerritt still waiting for decent earth to
hide her. As she thought – her underlip caught up by one
faded canine, brows knit and nostrils wide – she wielded the
poker with lunges that jarred the grating at the bottom, and
careful scrapes round the brick-work above. She looked at her
wrist-watch. It was getting on to half-past four, and the rain
was coming down in earnest. Tea would be at five. If It did not
die before that time, she would be soaked and would have to
change. Meantime, and this occupied her, Wynn's things were
burning well in spite of the hissing wet, though now and again
a book-back with a quite distinguishable title would be
heaved up out of the mass. The exercise of stoking had given
her a glow which seemed to reach to the marrow of her bones.
She hummed – Mary never had a voice – to herself. She had
never believed in all those advanced views – though Miss
Fowler herself leaned a little that way – of woman's work in
the world; but now she saw there was much to be said for
them. This, for instance, was her work – work which no man,
least of all Dr. Hennis, would ever have done. A man, at such a
crisis, would be what Wynn called a 'sportsman'; would leave
everything to fetch help, and would certainly bring It into the
house. Now a woman's business was to make a happy home
for – for a husband and children. Failing these – it was not a
thing one should allow one's mind to dwell upon – but – –

'Stop it!' Mary cried once more across the shadows. 'Nein, I tell you! Ich haben der todt Kinder gesehn.'

But it was a fact. A woman who had missed these things could still be useful–more useful than a man in certain respects. She thumped like a paviour through the settling ashes at the secret thrill of it. The rain was damping the fire, but she could feel – it was too dark to see – that her work was done. There was a dull red glow at the bottom of the destructor, not enough to char the wooden lid if she slipped it half over against the driving wet. This arranged, she leaned on the poker and waited, while an increasing rapture laid hold on her. She ceased to think. She gave herself up to feel. Her long pleasure was broken by a sound that she had waited for in agony several times in her life. She leaned forward and listened, smiling. There could be no mistake. She closed her eyes and drank it in. Once it ceased abruptly.

'Go on,' she murmured, half aloud. 'That isn't the end.'

Then the end came very distinctly in a lull between two rain-gusts. Mary Postgate drew her breath short between her teeth and shivered from head to foot. 'That's all right,' said she contentedly, and went up to the house, where she scandalised the whole routine by taking a luxurious hot bath before tea, and came down looking, as Miss Fowler said when she saw her lying all relaxed on the other sofa, 'quite handsome!'

12

Twenty-First Century Aunts

Seth is my nephew. His mother is my sister and his father is my brother-in law. Seth's conception took place in a Harley Street clinic Petri dish; the sperm was my brother-in-law's, and the egg was mine. He looks very like his father and shares his dashing eccentric style in clothes and sense of humour; nevertheless, he reminds us all of my son Peter when he was Seth's age.

My sister Flora asked me to give her an egg, and I was pleased she did. She and my brother-in-law Hugh had experienced eight years of disappointment which culminated in the devastating stillbirth of their naturally conceived daughter. By the time Flora and I had our first conversation about egg donation, Mark, my husband, and I considered every way we might help them get a baby, including having one and giving it to them. Now that we had heard about egg donation it seemed a very simple and natural thing to do for my sister, who in a great many ways had brought me up since I was fifteen.

She was a strikingly sharp child who delighted my father, who called her his 'Queen'. Until I was born she was the only girl amongst three boys, and her supremacy was unassailed. When she was told without any warning, aged five, that she had a sister upstairs, she said, 'How nice for me.' This was much quoted by my father and I always felt the ambivalence of the story. My sister guarded her position like a tiger, and I turned out not to be very nice for any of them, sneaking on my siblings and throwing tantrums whenever they teased me.

Until I was fifteen I lived in the shadow of my sister's brilliant, rebellious school career and her powerful presence at home. We were opposites: physically I began by being tall and strong for my age (I was christened Tamara Press by my siblings after a Russian weightlifter who was caught taking steroids), whereas Flora was wraith-like and grew into a teenage beauty. I charged about on my pony and Flora read in her room, eschewing any form of physical activity. Whereas she was naughty and quick, I was eager to please, and if I hadn't later been 'saved' by her, I may have ended up forever getting ready for my next gymkhana. I was both scared and immensely proud of her, and I longed to be like her but would be seized by jealous rages, hurling her (and anybody else's) things out of the window or pouring mince into her boyfriend's boots. Sometimes I would sneak into her room to try on one of her beautiful shoplifted dresses from Biba and get stuck, slightly wrecking them.

Flora then took my education in hand; she gave me a copy of The Female Eunuch, *introduced me to her radical friends and encouraged me in my sexual adventures. When our father died, we curled up in a bed together and slept through the wretched afternoon. After Dad's death, we spent a long time together going over and over our parents' unhappy marriage and how it had affected us. I turned out to be a lackadaisical feminist; although committed in spirit, I was lazy. I slept through university lectures and arrived in London with no degree or clue as to how I was to earn my living. By contrast, Flora was working hard as a criminal defence barrister in radical chambers. Never without a man in her life, she swore she would never have children and certainly never get married. When I rang to tell her I was going to have a baby, her comment was, 'I expect you're going to make a career of this.' She was and is a fabulous aunt, and our sons are extremely close to her and Hugh.*

If I, Mark, Flora and Hugh had not remained so close through their long efforts to get pregnant, especially during their pregnancy and its terrible end with the prenatal death of their baby girl, Dora, Seth's story might have been less straightforward. As it was, none of us could think of any reason to give the psychologist at the clinic as to why we shouldn't do it. Quite soon after we'd all agreed to give egg donation a try, Flora and Hugh looked into adoption and were given a three-month-old girl, Melody, to be their daughter. Her arrival was momentous and we were all ravished by her. The ghastliness of the death of Dora, Flora and Hugh's baby, and the awful years of unsuccessful fertility treatment were over. Somehow Melody made sense of it all. Flora and Hugh's adoration of her was marvellous to see and they took to her nurturing with easy confidence and joy. When not long after Melody's arrival Flora suggested that we go ahead with the egg donation, I reacted powerfully against it. Instead of feeling excited about the process, as I had done previously, it became unreasonably menacing. I found the prospect of the physical intrusion threatening, whereas before it had been insignificant. Also I became intractable over dates. It must have seemed very peculiar, as I hadn't really got much to do, except a show of my paintings that was coming up. I had always been cavalier about my health, consuming anything going. I think I behaved like this because it was too soon to revisit the traumas that Melody had put behind us, but I didn't quite realize it at the time.

It was a good thing to have delayed it, for we all agreed later that Melody's place in the world would certainly have been undermined had Flora fallen pregnant shortly after Melody's arrival. Flora and Hugh accepted my contrariness with great understanding; they didn't mention eggs again until Melody became such an integral part of all our lives that we could barely remember life without her. This time the atmosphere was different; Flora and Hugh had Melody, we agreed we were going to attempt one cycle to produce this baby and all desperation disappeared. It was exciting. Our visits to the psychologist and the clinic were made in this spirit. It felt as if we were watching ourselves in a Woody Allen movie as the four of us sat in a row in front of the psychologist, who tried to puzzle out whether this was going to end in disaster. There was a sense of unreality about it: I don't think any of us believed, or dared hope, it would result in a baby; besides which, the doctors made us feel as though we were part of an experiment in eugenics and gave us frightful giggles.

Though I hate needles, Mark got so good at giving me injections in my bottom that I didn't mind. The clinic made a mistake and overstimulated my ovaries and then wanted to scrap the procedure. I felt furious with them, as it seemed to prove their lack of humane interest in our case. It would have been very dispiriting for everyone to have to begin again, so we insisted on carrying on. The day of the beginning of Seth's conception was bizarre and very moving. As I staggered down the corridor to the theatre where the eggs were to be harvested (because of their miscalculation, I had so many in my ovaries it was uncomfortable to walk or sit up), I turned back to wave at Flora in the hall and to Hugh, who was climbing the stairs, with great dignity, to the room where he was to produce the sperm.

Three days later, three fertilized eggs were placed in Flora's womb; five others were put in a deep freeze. Flora's pregnancy had the same wonder about it as the Virgin Mary's – except, unlike Mary, we never got over our disbelief, even when we looked at the scan and could clearly see a boy. The closer it came to Seth's birth, the more incredible it became. Waiting at the hospital on the day of Seth's birth, while Flora and Hugh were in the operating theatre (it was a Caesarean section to mini-mize risk, so I was not allowed to be with them), was an agony of anxiety. I had sat with them during the stillbirth of Dora in the same hospital and was fully expecting to go through the same experience. I think we all were. It was impossible to sepa-rate the happiness from relief when Hugh finally appeared to tell me that Seth and Flora were safe and well.

Today our family have just got back from Seth's fourth birth-day party. Flora had cooked a delicious tea for Seth and his guests; she had made him a Thunderbird 2 cake. Seth is crazy about Thunderbird 2. Flora and Hugh made the party fun, warm and hospitable for us all, and everyone, especially Seth, surrounded by his friends and lovingly presided over by Melody, who is now six, had a lovely time.

When Flora approached the clinic to instigate the donation, the consultant was anxious about our being siblings. For me, it has made it beautifully simple: we share the same genes, so the way Flora does things is familiar – her cooking (which we both assimilated from our mother), the chaos we share in our sepa-rate houses, ideas about a good day out – and I know her great sense of humour, her outspokenness, her great pleasure in things. Both Mark and I love Hugh very much and admire and respect him, not least for the incredible support he gave Flora in her pursuit of children. (Hugh had mumps when he was nineteen and so wasn't figuring to have any children.) If I had any doubt that Seth and Melody were not being so fully loved and cared for in every way, I should be overwrought by it, and in Seth's case resentful and angry. But I was convinced that with Flora and Hugh this scenario would never happen. I am aware too that if I didn't love and respect Hugh I would have felt anxious about entering into our new relationship and then the joy of its success might have been awkward.

Flora and I have survived a quarrel since then; not a polite one either but a real fight in the style of our childhood, Flora torpedoing me with well-aimed missiles and then it ending up with me throwing a punch. It was a bit shocking for everyone – especially Mark and Hugh, who had not witnessed us in our childhood roles before. We got over it though.

I don't feel any more maternal for Seth than I do for Melody, but when I am with him I do feel very happy that I could help in his beginnings. While Flora was pregnant, the four of us had a conversation about whether the identity of Seth's biological mother should be out in the open or whether Seth should be able to choose whether he wants his origins to be out in the open. It has become open knowledge, and it would have been strange had it been otherwise, as theirs is a house without taboos. Still, after Seth was born and for his first couple of years, I stood back a little more than I might have done had I not thought there was a danger of Flora feeling I was hovering about too much. Now, Melody and Seth often come over to our house and spend the day with us, and we spend weekends at their house in the country. One day, when I was driving them over to my house, Melody said from the back, 'Emma, you know, Seth and I both have two mothers. I have my mother and Flora is my mother, and Seth has you and Flora is his mother too.' It was said with absolute certainty and without a trace of confusion. I looked round and Seth was nodding his head and grinning.

DOM ASHTON ON HIS AUNT DEB

Deb has been a famous theatre and opera director ever since I can remember. How would I describe her? Warm and exciting, friendly if she wants to be friendly and bossy when she needs to be bossy. She attracts attention wherever she goes. She's not very domesticated: she doesn't cook, but she enjoys cleaning occasionally. She won't even pick up the phone unless she absolutely has to, but she's a very good texter and always replies very fast. She is very driven and very, very good fun.

My dad is a transport consultant, my mum a garden designer. We live in Hampshire, though I was brought up for the first five years of my life in Hong Kong and Wimbledon. Now I'm in my first year of university at Nottingham, reading history. I've got one brother, Lysander, who's five years older than I am. We both went to Bedales, which I loved. He read physics at Bristol and is now in the film business. He and I aren't alike at all – sport and things like that are alien to him. I play football and hockey and do some martial arts. We're both into theatre, but he's always been more interested in the technical side, while I enjoy performing.

Deb came out to see us when we lived in Hong Kong, but what I remember more vividly, from the age of about seven, is going to stay with her for a couple of nights, on my own, at her flat in Primrose Hill, something which I've done regularly ever since. Now I can stay there even if she's not around.

We always have fun. When I was a kid, she used to let me eat ice cream in bed, and when I got a bit older we started going to lovely restaurants – sometimes posh ones like the Ivy, sometimes ordinary ones like Wagamama and Yo! Sushi. She also took me to the theatre, often to shows that she'd directed.

She did similar things with my brother and my cousin Leo, who's a computer graphic designer, the son of my Uncle Simon, Deb's and mum's elder brother. I don't think I'm her favourite. She's very even-handed, but I'm the youngest, which I suppose has made a bit of a difference. She really did spoil us, but it wasn't anarchy. She certainly wouldn't let us get up to every-thing we wanted to, certainly not, but fortunately we're quite well disciplined anyway. We had a few rows when I was younger, but not major ones. Usually they were about trivial things, like when she told me to ask a shop assistant something. For some reason, I didn't want to do this and it could some-times lead to arguments, particularly on our travels.

We talk about everything, especially matters relating to my family. I'm as open with her as I am with my mother. Unless I decided to join the army, she'd be very happy to support me in whatever I might decide to do. I thought for a time that I might go into the law, though it's an idea I'm now going off by the second.

Her work is very much part of our relationship, because she doesn't separate it from her life. We talk about it a lot, and I see virtually everything she does. The first thing I saw was at the Salzburg Festival when I was about ten – her production of Coriolanus. *Then there was* Don Giovanni *at Glyndebourne, but I'm not such a big opera fan. Perhaps I love the plays she directs more –* Medea, *which I saw in New York, and* The Powerbook *too. She was very nice about taking an interest in the plays I was in at Bedales. When I was Horatio in* Hamlet, *she went through the text with me, which was a great help. It was a great pity she couldn't come to a performance.*

She's amazingly good at presents. This Christmas she gave me a couple of very fashionable T-shirts, but usually her gifts involve trips somewhere. She gave me Eurostar vouchers when the tunnel first opened, and we went to Paris together for three days. I was about eleven, and it was all so new that it was extra exciting. We did all the touristy things, like going to the Eiffel

Tower and the Stade de France, and then we went out to dinner with Juliette Binoche. She often takes me along when she's meeting people. They're not business lunches exactly, but meetings with people she needs to stay in touch with for professional reasons.

We've been to Greece four times. She's got a friend, a theatre designer called Chloe, who has a house on Hydra, an island near Athens. This year we flew to Venice first and then took the ferry. It took thirty hours on a pretty grotty boat. We slept on the floor, but it was fun. Once we're in Greece, we tend to laze about in the sun reading or we swim and snorkel, and there's always lots of talking and eating.

New York was another great trip. I hadn't been there before. We went up the World Trade Center, stayed in a flashy hotel called the Hudson, had dinner at the River Café and at my request went to see The Rocky Horror Show.

Perhaps the best birthday present was being an extra in her film The Last September. *I went over to Ireland for five days of the shooting. My finest moment is when you can see me running in front of Maggie Smith at a garden party. I am in the background in about five other scenes – a bit of favouritism, I guess! My brother Lysander didn't get to be in the film, but instead Deb flew him out to New York to be her companion at the Tony awards, when she was nominated for* Medea.

I think Deb and my mum were close when they were children. There's a four-year age gap between them, my mother being the elder. My relationship to Deb is very different from the one I had with my mother – she's got the harder day-to-day job, I suppose. I tend to see Deb when it's a special occasion like a birthday or when we do lovely things together.

She has taught me some important lessons in life. Her people skills are brilliant; the way she can get on with anyone is amazing. The other day we got a free panettone in a restaurant in Primrose Hill because of the way she was joking with the waiters. She has also shown me how to get something done when it needs to be done.

I have another blood aunt. She's my father's sister Philida. She's in her sixties and is really extremely nice but basically a family person. She leads a different life from Deb's, and we tend to meet up with her at family get-togethers, which Deb can't always make. But as Philida has her own children, I've spent much less one-on-one time with her. And I suppose that's what it comes down to: one main reason that Deb's relationship with her nephews is so unique and exciting is that she hasn't got any children of her own.

Mercy Barrett on her Aunt Nerine

My aunt gives me presents and she hugs me so hard that I can hardly breathe. I wish I saw her all the time, but she went back to live in Jamaica, so I only see her when we go on holiday there. She is tall and quite fat, and she loves singing, cooking, cleaning the house and watching videos. When she laughs you can see she has hundreds of teeth. Her house is made of wood, and it smells of wood and burnt things. Her daughter is called Susan, who is nearly the same age as me. She is my cousin and also one of my best friends, and we send each other letters and postcards. She is at a convent called Sacred Heart of Jesus in a place called Mona. There are real nuns there. My school is

called Sacred Heart of Jesus too, but it isn't a convent and the teachers are ordinary people.

For my birthday Auntie Nerine sent me an orange dress with blue bits and pictures of trees and leaves and things on it. I can't remember what she gave me for Christmas, but I am sure it was nice.

My dad has gone away and we don't know when he'll come back. I do miss him, but I love being at home with my mam and sisters. Sometimes we talk to Auntie Nerine on the telephone on Sundays after we go to church, and I say a prayer for her at night. Maybe she will come to England again soon. I wish I could see her now, I really do. I have another aunt called Paulette who lives in Wembley, but I don't think Mam likes her, so we don't see her that much. She didn't send me a present for my birthday, which aunts are always meant to do.

13

The Good Aunt Guide

MRS GEORGE WEMYSS, *The Professional Aunt* (1919)

As the children grow older the duties of the aunt become more arduous. For the benefit of schoolboy nephews with exeats, she must have an intimate acquaintance with the Hippodrome, any exhibition going, every place of instruction of a kind, or amusement. She must be thoroughly up in matinees, and know what plays are frightfully exciting, and she must have a nice taste in sweets. She need not necessarily eat them, it is perhaps better if she does not. But she must know where the very best are to be procured. She must never get tired. She must love driving in hansoms and going on the top of buses. She must know where the white ones go, and where the red ones don't, although a mistake on her part is readily forgiven if it prolongs the drive without curtailing a performance of any kind. This requires great experience. She must set aside, moreover, a goodly sum every year for professional expenses.

MEET AUNT POLLY, A PAGE ON dearauntpolly.com

When Aunt Polly meets you, she doesn't care how you speak or what kind of grades you have. You are special to her, and she accepts you exactly as you are. Somehow, her acceptance inspires you to be yourself and to be your best. You dare to try different paths until you find your own. Along the way, you learn to respect the people and land and animals around you. If you have a problem, Aunt Polly has a story or a song to help you think about it. She can find something to laugh about in almost any situation, and if she can't, she will comfort you in a deep way, underneath the tears.

Aunt Polly seems like a country aunt because she loves nature and the seasons and the quiet of a rural morning. She lives a slower pace, and she always has time for tea. Her old house and rambling garden and the people in her town are very important to her. But Aunt Polly also keeps a bag packed under the stairs, just in case she has a last minute chance to travel. She has seen the desert and the ocean. She appreci- ates that there are whole separate worlds on every street. She loves to walk and watch the people, listen to their languages and learn their ways. Aunt Polly knows how to bring a little country to the city and a little city to the country and they both seem better for it when she is there.

In many ways, Aunt Polly seems young – always ready to play a game, hike a mountain, try something new. But she still believes in some of the old ways. Not just the old-fashioned milk-and-cookie ways, but the ways of the days gone by, when the elders held a place of honor by the fire and the children were proud to serve them. Sometimes, after sunset, when Aunt Polly lights a candle and sits on the porch and tells stories, it seems like you are part of an ancient tribe and you want to dance and sing.

The Golden Rules for Aunts

Always talk up to the niece or nephew and assume they are slightly older than they are.

Find out what the n. or n.'s interests are, and listen to them without interruption.

Tell them about your own life, and what it's like to be you – they may not register immediately, but it will sink in.

Presents don't have to be big or expensive, but they should be imaginative – and arrive on the right day.

Outings: follow the n. or n.'s enthusiasms, but don't fake yours. You may want to go and revisit your childhood at *The Nutcracker* – the n. or n. would probably prefer the latest blockbuster movie. Compromise by trying something new to both of you, and make it an adventure.

Get the n. or n. away from their parents, and see them on their own.

School is most children's favourite topic of conversation. Don't forget what their best subject is or the name of their most loathed teacher.

Don't be too cosy. Aunts should expand the n. or n.'s range of experience.

Be fun, but don't try to be funny. Your idea of a joke will not be theirs and all attempts to be 'with it' will be instantly unmasked, leaving you branded as a phoney.

Don't, please, remark how the n. or n. has grown since you last saw them. It's jolly irritating, remember?

The Golden Rules for Nieces and Nephews

Don't assume that you are the most important thing in her life.

A thank-you letter or message – by telephone or email, if not by post – is due for every gift or outing.

Remember your aunt's birthday, as she remembers yours.

Remember that she's getting old, but don't remind her of it.

Tease her as much as you like, but don't call her 'aunt' or 'auntie' if she really doesn't like it.

Keep in touch.

Acknowledgements

I am indebted to an enormous number of friends and acquaintances who have contributed aunts and ideas to this book. Notable among them are Angela Abdesallam, Juliet Annan, Michael Arditti, Dominic Ashton, Ariane Bankes, Henrietta Bredin, Hattie Dorment, Stéphanie Falcoz, Flossie Joll, Jonathan Keates, Lauro Martines, Robert Maxtone-Graham, Ysenda Maxtone-Smith, Gerald Martin Moore, Gley Moreno, Caroline Muir, Val Newby, Virginia Nicholson, Nicky Normanby, Sam Organ, Angus Robb, Felicity Rubinstein, Isabella de Sabata, Miranda Seymour, Adam Sisman, Lucinda Stevens, Gill Sutherland, Zoe Svendsen, Robert Turnbull, Deborah Warner, Giles Waterfield, Ann Webb, Katharine Whitehorn and Cristina Zilkha. My gratitude to the staff at the British Library and London Library, and to Tim Berners-Lee, whose invention of the internet has transformed the possibilities of researching a book such as this.

Special thanks, as always, to my inspirational agent Caroline Dawnay; to my late mother Kate Christiansen, who gave me great encouragement at the outset; and to Candia McWilliam, whose sharp and sensitive eye saved me from solecisms. Claire Pamment, Rachel Sussman and Henrietta Bredin helped most effectively with research. At Faber, my marvellous editor Belinda Matthews has been – in perfectly judged balance – a constant support and occasional goad.

Some names in the text have been changed.

Photographs: p. 16, photographer unknown; p. 84, National Portrait Gallery (Ramsay and Muspratt); p. 210, Thomas Woods; p. 256, Caroline Obolensky.

Rachel Townsend's piece on her Aunt Emily Caroline Kington-Blair-Oliphant of Ardblair was reproduced from a privately published pamphlet by kind permission of her family. For permission to quote, thanks are also due to Persephone Books ('Aunts' by Virginia Graham, an extract from *Consider the Years*, re-published by Persephone, 2000); the William Plomer Trust (extracts from *Curious Relations*); Lupus Music (Syd Barrett's lyric 'Gigolo Aunts'); Society of Authors (extracts from Virginia Woolf's diaries); and Taylor and Francis Books UK ('The Story of Seth's Egg', an extract from *Inconceivable Conceptions*, edited by Juliet Miller and Jane Haynes, 2003).

OKANAGAN REGIONAL LIBRARY
3 3132 02914 6075